TO: Steve

Laura Doucet

May God Bless Your Soul!.!.

Love You!!!!

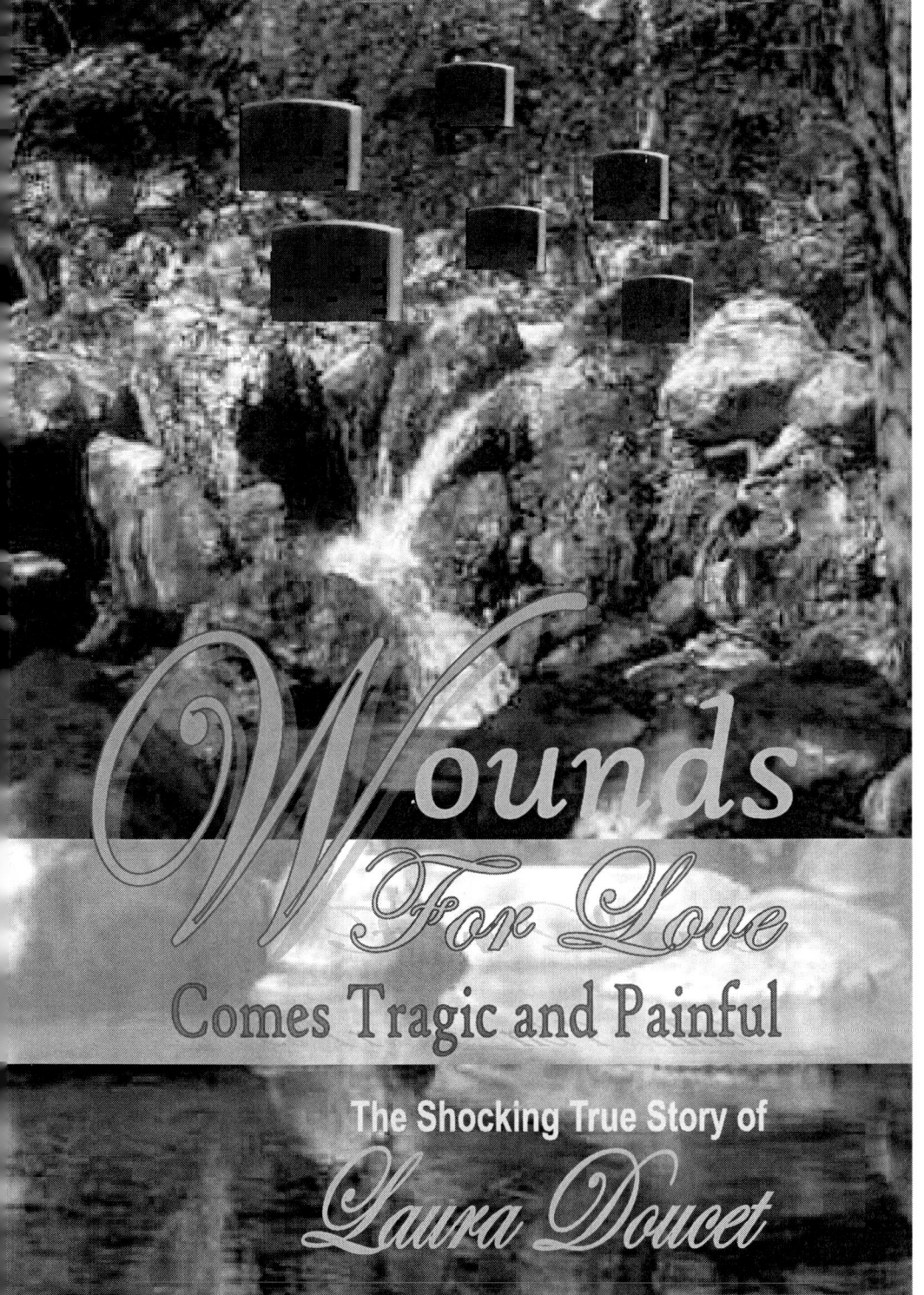

WOUNDS: For Love Comes Tragic and Painful
The Shocking True Story of
Laura Doucet

Published by Laura Doucet
Printed in the U.S.A.
Copyright 2012. All Rights Reserved.

Contributing Writer & Editor
Consultant Merle Ray
www.MyBestSeller.org
www.NobleGroups.com
www.MerleRay.com
(281) 827-4396

Audio Book by Laura Doucet and Merle Ray
Voice-over Artist, Katherine Claudette Campbell at
www.KatherineClaudette.com

ISBN: 978-0-9852285-0-7

All rights reserved. No part of this book may be reproduced or transmitted in any form or by any means, electronic or mechanical, including photocopy, recording, or by any information storage and retrieval system, without written permission from the author.

Unless otherwise indicated, Bible quotations are taken from The Holy Bible King James Version, Public Domain.

WOUNDS
For Love Comes Tragic and Painful
The Shocking True Story of Laura Doucet

CONTENTS

Introduction
Cutting Myself with Stones 9
    A Message to My Readers 11

Growing Up 12
    Dad's Family 13
    Mom's Family 24
    Mom 28
    The Twins 32
    The Old Country Road 37

Virgin Bride 41
    The Perfect Wedding 47

Let He who is Without Sin 55
Cast the First Stone 97
Live to Tell 104
Rolling Away the Stone 121
Wounded For Me – *About the Author* 125

WOUNDS
FOR LOVE COMES TRAGIC AND PAINFUL

This story is based on actual events in my life. All dates, places, and times in this account are factual and represent to the best of my ability the facts as I remember them. Most names of characters have been changed in order to protect the innocent and respect the privacy of individuals. God knows it is not my intent to misrepresent or omit anyone's character in my story or overlook their contributions to my life and this work. Any omission or misprint is fully mine to accept and purely made by mistake. I ask for your forgiveness and support in advance, as I continue on in my journey of healing.

DEDICATION

To My Dad

And always, night and day, she was in the mountains, and in the tombs, crying, and cutting herself with **stones.**
Mark 5:5

Let him who is without sin cast the first **stone.**
John 8:7

*And they said among themselves,
Who shall roll us away the* **stone**
*from the door of the grave?
And when they looked,
they saw that the* **stone** *was rolled away.*
Mark 16:2-4

Introduction
Cutting Myself with Stones

Like any other kids we got our share of ass whippings, and like any other kid I hated getting my ass whipped. In my household you learned that if you did the crime, then you had to do the time – there was a price to be paid for disobedience. I remember when I was about fifteen or sixteen years old and we had a phone in the house. In the 60's living in the country, folks didn't always have a phone. I remember my brother and sisters were playing outside with my dad, and my mom was gone to the store in town.

Mom had been gone for about twenty minutes when the phone rang. I answered the phone but no one said anything, so I hung up. It rang again and I answered the phone again, but they didn't say anything. So before I hung up this time, I hollered the "B" *word* and hung up. I thought someone was playing around with the phone. What I didn't know was that my mother was trying to call the house and she was having trouble with the call. I recall being so scared because I didn't know what my mother was going to do to me. After my mother got done telling me that she doesn't use words like that, or for that matter,

Wounds
For Love Comes Tragic and Painful

curse at all, I knew I had trouble coming. I had never heard my mother curse or use profanity of any kind, but that day, she was mad as hell. I never wanted to disappoint my mom again – not because I was afraid of getting a whipping, but because I couldn't stand the thought of my mother being disappointed in me. That day I promised myself I would never see that look on my mother's face again. I would never cause her pain.

But I did. I brought the whole family pain. Because of me, my dad was dead and gone. For 30 years, I had suppressed the pain and anguish of losing my father, and taking away the man me, my mother, sisters, and brother loved so dearly. The horrifying memory of his death was being played over and over again in my mind like a scratched up song being played on a CD. The look on my mother's face when I told her what happened, and the scream I heard from Mom in the emergency room as the surgeon told us my dad didn't make it, were all plastered on the walls of rooms inside my mind. They were the new furniture inside my soul, the place where all my dreams, hopes, imaginations, and desires lived. My soul was the place where I had expected a great life with my new husband – the tall young handsome man that I had dated so happily for three years and remained a virgin until our wedding night. Now that same soul was torturing me; the memories that lived there were causing me pain, so much pain that I could not go on. I just wanted to die, and die I tried.

A MESSAGE TO MY READERS

Throughout this book, in my broken English and Cajun Creole French dialect you will hear me say, "I recall," or "I remember." Please do not become frustrated at the many times you will hear those words. Understand that my healing is taking place. At the cemetery where they buried my father, I buried my memories. All of them, the good ones and the bad, so that after many years I could not even remember much. I blocked out my childhood. For too long, these memories have been buried underneath the tombstone of my mind weighing down on my thoughts, ideas, imaginations, and desires. I buried my memories so deep that I have yet to tell my story.

Well today, I have lived to tell, and tell I will so that some other young person and family may be spared from the tragedy and pain that I suffered at the hands of the wounded soul who stoned me.

GROWING UP

I was a born in 1962 in Lafayette, Louisiana and raised by my parents in a small town called Ville Platte. My mom and dad were both seventeen at the time they married, except Dad was a few months older than my mom. Back then folks not only got married at a very young age, they had children early on in their marriage. My mom had me when she was eighteen years old. She was very sick, not just when she was pregnant, but before and after that.

Over the years I was told that my mom had an illness called TB, but I didn't know anything about TB. All I knew is that she was sick a lot. I was told that I was sent home from the hospital with my dad's mom, Grandma Bee, who I called Memét. She had to take care of me. My mom was hospitalized for many months after I was born, and I feel I never got to bond with her as a newborn usually bonds with its mother. Because of this, as a young child, I had more distinct memories of my grandparents, uncles, and aunts than I did of spending time with my parents. All I remember is my dad taking my mom to different doctors when I was younger, but I still didn't know or understand what was wrong with my mom. My mom continued to be sick throughout the years. As I got a little older, I recall my mom telling me and my siblings one day after she had been in the hospital for so long that when the doctors gave her a pass this time to come home for the Thanksgiving holidays, she was never going back to that hospital.

Growing up with my family being so close to my grandparents, I had a lot of uncles and aunts who helped to care for me on both sides of the family. I was told by one of my uncles that he had to babysit me, even though he wanted to go out for the night. I was the oldest child of my parents and the oldest grandchild in the family. At the time I was born, my dad was farming with his family to make ends meet. My parents didn't finish school. Dad quit in the sixth grade to help his family with the farming, and Mom was unable to finish. She was sick for so long that she had fallen way behind in her school work, so she stopped in the eighth grade. Both my mom's father and my dad's father were farmers in agriculture. They were so good at it that I had no idea they had little to no education until I was nearly grown.

DAD'S FAMILY

My Grandfather, Pappá Cliff, was a blacksmith and he had his own tool shop. Back then one thing black folks didn't need was for their tools to be dull while they were working the fields and doing all the

WOUNDS
FOR LOVE COMES TRAGIC AND PAINFUL

other types of handiwork they had to do. They used all kinds of knives, axes, and other types of tools used for farming. Pappá Cliff was also a carpenter on top of being a welder. Even though he had no educational background, God had blessed him and his family with so many gifts and talents. I had always thought it so amazing that my grandparents on both my mom's and dad's side had no education, yet they had trades for business and much more. I was very proud of my family because they didn't let being poor stop them. My family members were quick learners. They never lost sight of their goals and they learned to get the job done. Back in the day, that was pretty good considering my family had to farm to make money, and they had other chores around the house as well. In their time, my family didn't have a phone not to mention a lot of other things they had to do without.

God not only blessed my family with many talents, God had blessed them with the gift of knowledge as well *to know how* to do things. Without the gift of knowledge, they didn't know anything. It was amazing to me that they knew how to make their own home remedies when someone was sick. They weren't able to go to the doctor all the time because their money had to be spent on other things like food, shelter, and clothing. Besides for a long time, the nearest doctor and hospital was over 45 minutes away

-Growing Up -

in Lafayette. So they had learned to make their own kind of medicine for their bodies.

My family and other families before them learned from their families before them. This knowledge of healing remedies, agriculture, welding, carpentry, and such had been passed on from generation to generation. All the families had to endure so much back then. Growing up in the 1920's, 30's, and 40's, my parents, grandparents, and great grandparents didn't have the same options or opportunities that I and my siblings had in the 70's, 80's, and 90's. Because of what they did back in those days, an easier way was made for me and my siblings. I know that my parents, grandparents, and their parents before them just wanted an opportunity to provide for their families and their children, so we and our children could have a better life. I thank God for my ancestors and others before them.

I was told later on in life that some of my ancestors were Indian. I noticed that some of my family members had long pretty black hair almost like white folks. Some of my family members could have even passed for white; they had fair pretty skin tone that I thought was so beautiful and soft. My family experienced so much back in those days and they had to work for so little. I remember being so shocked

WOUNDS
FOR LOVE COMES TRAGIC AND PAINFUL

when my parents told me and my siblings how much things cost and how they had to work for so little. I was told by my grandparents that our ancestors before them had to endure slavery, racism, segregation, rape, and working in the fields from sun up to sun down picking cotton, sugar cane, and potatoes for little of nothing. Being black and poor, they did what they had to in order to survive the white rules. I must have come from a very strong line of ancestors. Make no mistake about it; I knew my family was far from being weak.

Therefore, I was a little disappointed when I found out that the house and the land that my grandparents lived on for so long wasn't theirs. They had been renting for all those years. Pappá Cliff was renting the house and using the land to farm on. In exchange for profit of the crop, he would pay the owner rent for the house and land when it was harvest time. The cost of food, rent and living expenses wasn't that much back then, but they got paid little to nothing. Sometimes they would only make four or five dollars a week to live off of.

My Memét, Pappá Cliff's wife, had a big family and she enjoyed cooking for her family, or I should she say – she enjoyed teaching her daughters how to do all the cooking. She believed in her children

- GROWING UP -

and she loved her family. Cooking was one of things the older generation loved to do and became very good at it. Memét loved feeding folk. When people would visit, she would always ask them if they were hungry, and then she would go about making sure they had plenty to eat right then. According to my aunts, Memét's daughters, Memét loved to make them do all the cooking while Memét would sit in her rocking chair on the porch. Memét loved sitting in that rocking chair with a big glass of cold water and ice. I believe that's the reason why I love rocking chairs myself because I saw her seated in hers every day rocking herself back and forth relaxing on the porch. I used to do a lot of thinking and daydreaming in that chair; it was calming to me. I remember my grandparents had a big porch. It was big enough to store wood for the two fireplaces in their house. Memét even had a cooler on the porch so we didn't have to go in and out of the kitchen to get water. They had to draw water from a well every day, and they would sit some in the cooler on the porch.

When family and friends would come home from out of town, it didn't matter what time of day or night it was; they were always welcome at Memét's house. It was like a hotel where you never had to worry about anything to eat or where to sleep. You were treated as guests. The funny thing about that is you didn't have to pay anything; you just would come

WOUNDS
FOR LOVE COMES TRAGIC AND PAINFUL

and have a good time. Memét, she would always make them feel welcome all the time. So yes! Louisianans are known for their Southern hospitality and good food. I am glad that is a part of my heritage.

There was one other thing about Memét – if any of her children were sick, or had something going wrong with them, she would get the family together and decide what they were going to do. She was the glue that held the family together. Pappá Cliff, her counterpart, was easy going, very calm. He wouldn't let anything worry him. Pappá Cliff was full of ideas, and he spoke with a very soft voice. He was a lot of fun. He was a very tall handsome man who loved to wear hats. He would also sit and relax on the porch while smoking his Bugle tobacco.

I remember my dad loved to wear his hats and smoke Bugle tobacco just like my Pappá. I used to watch when they would roll up their Bugle tobacco; that was the brand that people smoked back then. Although there was a time when I couldn't even stand the smell of cigarette smoke, I savor the memory of that smell today because it reminds me of the two men that I have loved the most in my lifetime, my Pappá and my dad.

-Growing Up-

I used to think my mother didn't like going over to my grandparents' house much. When we would go with her, she never would want to stay long, and she used to always fuss at us about not getting dirty. The house was off a long dirt road where nothing but land, grass, and dirt was all around. My grandparents had lived there over forty years since my Uncle Nick was about two or three months old. They had a big family of fourteen people in that house - six boys and six girls with Pappá Cliff and Memét. They were a close knit family, and I felt they were always there for each other.

Dad was a tall handsome young man with a beard. He always had a smile on his face. He loved helping people and like his family, he was always there for them when they needed him. That was just his nature – helping people. He loved talking to anyone; it didn't matter what color you were. He loved to smile and make others laugh; he also loved to dance; he was a very outgoing person, and he loved spending time with his family.

His family was his life. Dad was Godfather to one of his twin sisters, Lynn. He had spoiled her. If she was in trouble, all she had to do was call him and he was there. It didn't matter how far she lived, he was always there for his sister. The same thing went

WOUNDS
FOR LOVE COMES TRAGIC AND PAINFUL

for his other sisters and brothers. All they had to do was call him, and he was there. My dad, his sisters, and his brothers loved to joke around. They would have so much fun when they got together; they would do nothing but have a good time laughing and joking around. Dad and his siblings loved to dance. Sometimes when we would visit our grandparents after church, we would have dinner, and they would dance all that Sunday afternoon until evening time came. They would turn the music on in the living room, and they would have a good time. I loved watching them dance, laugh, and tell jokes to each other. My best memories are of being around them when I was a young girl.

When I was growing up, I loved to hear the different stories my aunts would tell me all the time. My aunts used to tell me jokes about my Memét that would have me laughing and crying at the same time. When I was around my Aunt Glenda and her sisters, there was never a dull moment. Even with the amount of work that they had to do daily, that did not stop them from telling me their stories. My Aunt Glenda and her sisters would tell me stories about everything that happened in the house, and some of them were ghost stories. They would tell me stories about my Memét, and how she would never get up out of her rocking chair, even get a glass of water, and how she loved to give them orders to do this and that.

-GROWING UP-

I will never forget the time when Aunt Glenda told me about her and her twin sister, Lynn planning to elope. Aunt Glenda made me laugh when she told me how she packed her bags and was ready to go on that Saturday night. But her twin, Aunt Lynn found out about what she was planning to do. Aunt Lynn didn't want Aunt Glenda to leave her behind, so a week later after Aunt Glenda eloped, Aunt Lynn then decided to elope too. Aunt Lynn was a beautiful young woman with long pretty black hair; she had beautiful soft skin and she had a figure like a model. Memét knew that whatever her daughter, Glenda was doing, she knew that her twin, Lynn was sure to follow within fifteen minutes later. That is how close they were to each other.

It was to fun to hear Aunt Glenda say that she climbed out of their bedroom window on a Saturday night. Aunt Glenda said that Memét found out the next day that she'd eloped and said that she didn't know she had a cow that could jump over the fence. When Aunt Glenda and her twin Lynn eloped, they moved to Houston and started new lives with their husbands. We also had several family members before them who had already moved to Houston to start a family and new lives together.

WOUNDS
FOR LOVE COMES TRAGIC AND PAINFUL

I knew that my aunts and uncles had much spunk, pride, integrity, and loyalty. Their word was their bond always. Our big family reminded me of Earl Hamners' old family television show, the Waltons. Our family had the same family values as The Waltons. If we could have had our own TV show, it would have been just like The Waltons, only the black version.

When Aunt Glenda and Aunt Lynn left home, they were the last to leave. All of the other siblings were much older and had left home already to start their own families. With the children gone, that still didn't stop Memét from cooking a big meal every week. She knew that one of her sons or daughters would come by sometime during the day or before the week was over, and she wanted to make sure she had enough food cooked for them. And even though my grandparents didn't have a phone, and they lived way out in the country, my grandparents always got new news before anyone else in the family did.

I can remember one Christmas holiday when Aunt Glenda and her twin, Lynn and their husbands came home for the holidays. Memét noticed that Aunt Lynn was very sick. Aunt Lynn told her mother that she had seen a doctor months before coming home. She told her mother that the doctor had

-GROWING UP-

examined her and gave her some medicine at the time for an infection, but clearly my Memét could see that there was something worrying her. It was her breasts. Though Aunt Lynn had already seen a doctor in Houston several months before, when she went back to see the doctor again, the doctor wouldn't see her because she didn't have any medical insurance at the time. Aunt Lynn said that she was still having problems with her breasts and that the doctor had just examined her outside. He didn't even run any tests on her; the doctor said that it was an infection. Memét insisted that she was taking her to see the family doctor in Louisiana after the holiday when the doctor's office was open again.

When Memét took Aunt Lynn to see her doctor in the country and he examined her, what he told my Memét wasn't good news. The doctor admitted Aunt Lynn into the hospital and had them run more tests to confirm what he thought was wrong with her. The doctor told Memét that Aunt Lynn had breast cancer in both her breasts and they would have to do surgery to remove both breasts because the cancer was spreading. The doctor told Memét that after the surgery, Aunt Lynn would undergo chemotherapy. Aunt Lynn soon underwent surgery and chemotherapy with many other challenges. She would be weak, tired, and lose her beautiful hair. She

Wounds
For Love Comes Tragic and Painful

went through many months with the cancer spreading to her lungs and finally pneumonia.

Over the years I watched a number of my loved ones battle this deadly disease. It affected Aunt Lynn at a very early age. She was only twenty-six when she left. In the following years, Memét also lost the fight to breast cancer. Several years later her oldest daughter, Alberta also ran a good race but lost the fight to cancer.

Mom's Family

My mom also came from a large family. My Grandma Amy, Mamáu, was mom's mother. She had fourteen children – eight girls and six boys. I was never sure what type of work her husband, my Grandpa John, did. I was told Grandpa John was sick for a long time and he died. I didn't remember him. Growing up I never heard my mom or her siblings talk much about their dad and that was kind of strange to me. I was always a curious person, and so I had a hard time with accepting the fact that they didn't know the cause of their father's death. I was simply told the cause of his death was unknown. I was also told that because Mamáu Amy had no education, it was very hard for her to understand what the doctor was telling her about Grandpa John.

-Growing Up-

There were so many things I didn't understand when they would talk about the doctor or their sicknesses. Mamáu Amy's English was not the best because she would talk mostly in French Creole, which is part of our culture, but I did not speak the language very well. It identifies a lot about who we are. I didn't come to know that until years later when I was much older and began to learn more about our French Creole descent in Louisiana. This unique language was a part of my heritage deep down in the swamps of Louisiana culture passed down from generation to generation by our ancestors. Good Cajun Creole food, and the best Cajun Zydeco music had become trademarks of this wonderful language which is a combination of broken English and French. Folks from all over the world have come to enjoy Cajun food and learn Zydeco music, doing dances like the two-step. Not only do we have a unique dialect, families from the Louisiana Cajun French Creole culture where I come from are a unique breed of people.

For example, one of the things I learned was that when Mom and some of her siblings were sick, I was told that they were all cured from the sicknesses they had. I was never told much about the sicknesses themselves though. I couldn't understand the reason families like ours kept their sicknesses or illnesses a secret for many years. Like the TB my mother had, it

Wounds
For Love Comes Tragic and Painful

was hard as a young child trying to understand what was going on with my mother.

I only knew over the years that my mother and some of her siblings were affected by this disease. It was kept a secret for so long that I was finally told years later that it was also what Grandpa John had. I didn't remember Grandpa John because he died when I was six years old. I learned that my Uncle John A and I were very close in age, as my mom and Mamáu Amy were both pregnant at the same time. I was not aware of how close I was to Uncle John A until years after he died.

After Grandpa John died, my Mamáu Amy focused on raising her children and she never remarried. She remained a widow until her death. My Mamáu loved all her children. She was a very loving person who talked a lot of shit; she was a feisty old woman. I believe my Mamáu was a true Frenchman! She loved having her independence. I remember one time when I was joking around with my Mamáu. I had asked her why she did not remarry. Her response was that she didn't need a man with a grin on her face, and then she would start rattling something off in French. Even though I didn't understand the French words she was saying, she would sound so funny that I couldn't help but laugh. Mamáu Amy

- GROWING UP -

was a down to earth person and she loved having fun with her grandchildren. Mamáu and her sister Irma were very close. Actually, they were like two peas in a pod. Everyone in the neighborhood loved these two old women. They talked more mess then anybody I knew. They loved to joke around and make people laugh and they loved drinking their morning coffee together while sitting on the porch.

My mom wasn't much of a talker or into Zydeco dancing like her mother. Mom was a shy and quiet person. Back then, she didn't smile much. Mom was more of a church-going woman. She was a woman who not only loved going to church, but she loved to serve God. As far as I can remember, when she was not hospitalized or at home sick, every Sunday morning Mom would turn on the radio listening to Gospel music. She would prepare our family dinner the night before church.

My parent's families were very close-knit. Even though they didn't have a lot, what they did have was enough, and that was the ability to share memories and love between sisters and brothers. That is one thing that cannot be bought. I have always admired that about my parent's families. The relationship that my parents had with their brothers and sisters is something that I always remembered

Wounds
For Love Comes Tragic and Painful

and hoped that one day when I got older, I and my sisters and brother would have relationships like theirs.

Mom

Even though Mom was physically sick a lot during my childhood, she showed her incredible strength by making a great home life for us when she was not hospitalized. While Dad was out in the field farming with his family trying to make a living, Mom was a housewife who saw to it that everything was running smoothly in the house. My mother was a very good cook and she wasn't just a mother and wife, she had skills like managing their finances. She loved working with her hands, sewing, quilting, and taking care of the household. I see my Mom as one of the strongest black women I have ever seen, not to mention she is a very beautiful woman with very soft skin and a nice body. She is the classiest woman I know. My mom is a woman of integrity, dignity, pride, strength, honor, courage, and honesty. I have come to love her for so many reasons.

Growing up, I felt my mother and I never had a very close relationship. To me, it just seemed that there was always a disconnect between us. Mom was always so quiet. I always felt a little intimidated by her, and I never knew what to say to her, especially

- GROWING UP -

when we were alone. Because my mother didn't smile much and she always had a serious look on her face, there were times when I thought that mother was a mean person. It was hard for me to tell because she was so reserved and a quiet person. I had always felt that maybe because of my mother's sickness, maybe that's why she often didn't smile or talk much. There were a lot of things in life that I didn't understand as I was getting older – things about myself and about my mother. I wanted my mother to explain those things to me, female things, and growing up things, but I was always too afraid to ask.

We had lots of family time where Mom and Dad would play different games with us and it seemed as though Mom was enjoying herself, but she still didn't smile much. There were times when I thought that Mom was mad at me, and I always felt that Mom was harder on me. I feel if we had talked more, then maybe we would have had a much better relationship and a stronger bond between us. I just didn't understand as a child how to get closer to my mom. I was always too afraid to talk to her then.

Growing up in our household, one thing I can say is that we had lots of fun with Mom and Dad together. Even though Mom was the quiet one and she didn't talk much, she was full of energy when we

WOUNDS
FOR LOVE COMES TRAGIC AND PAINFUL

would play together as a family. It was as if she loved that even though she didn't show it. At times I would catch Mom enjoying herself, but she would try to play it off, like she was not enjoying herself. I even noticed every now and then Mom would enjoy a dance or two with Dad. I always enjoyed watching them. We knew Mom wasn't much of a dancer. I wasn't either, but I loved to watch them. That was one of the ways we learned to entertain ourselves in our home. So even though Mom was always sick, she never let that keep her from raising her family. She was a very strong person.

One of my most fond memories is of going to church. Because of my mom's passion for church, I loved going to church too. Maybe that was one of the few ways I could feel closer to Mom, I don't know. Mom never missed a Sunday morning without listening to her Gospel music early while she was cooking. My mother always prepared our Sunday dinner before going to church. That's the way most women did back then, so when they came home from church, their food would already be cooked. All they had to do was warm it up. Women back then also fixed their men's food on the plate and brought it to them if they were not sitting at the dinner table. Women didn't mind serving men and children back then. Whatever they needed at home, work, or school, the women would figure out a way to get it done.

-Growing Up-

I loved those Sundays most of all. My sisters and I were singing in the choir and although some of my siblings would complain to Mom about having to go to church, she never had to ask me twice. I loved singing in the choir, not to mention the revivals. That was some good church going on! Folks did more praying and singing those old hymn songs more than anything else. Back then, folks were afraid of God's wrath upon them or their children, so they took God's word very seriously for their lives. They would go to church, listen to their preachers, and try to do what's right by one another, treating everybody like they wanted to be treated.

That is one thing about me, if I was wrong, I didn't mind admitting that I was wrong even as a child. But if I was right, I would also let you know that too. I can remember how my siblings and I didn't always get along. We fussed about everything, but we loved each other. There were times when we would be angry at each other, and my mom would tell us that must be the way we show our love for each other, fussing, and she was right.

Like I said before, I could never let my mom down. I developed a deep respect for my mom over the years. Aside from cursing on the phone that time to her, I remember one time when everyone else was

WOUNDS
FOR LOVE COMES TRAGIC AND PAINFUL

gone, and Mom and I were at the house alone. My mom asked me why I never had much to say to her, and I remember telling her, *"I just don't know what to say to you."* My mom got angry at me for saying that and she didn't say anything else to me all day. So I learned not to share much thinking with my mom because I didn't want to make a mistake and hurt her feelings again. It just seemed that little stuff like that made it uncomfortable and difficult for me to relate and bond with my mom. Little did I realize that was just the beginning of our challenges bonding with each other. Time would bring about a change that neither one of us could prepare for.

THE TWINS

I was the oldest of my siblings, raised with my brother and three sisters up until the time Mom had the twins in 1975. I was thirteen years old at the time when my mother was pregnant. My sisters, my brother, and I were so excited that we could hardly wait until the babies got here. There were already five of us and now twins will make it seven. I remember Mom being sick throughout her pregnancy, and she was having a hard time. Mom said she and Dad went to the doctor and the doctor told them that she was pregnant. Mom said she wasn't planning to have any more children. My baby sister was eight years old at the time. Mom said when she went back for her

-GROWING UP-

checkup, the doctor told them that she was having twins and she fainted at the doctor's office.

The twins finally came in October 1975. Even though they were not identical twins, Mom named them similar names and she wanted to make sure that the twins didn't have nicknames. Back then, folks had nicknames that they used so much, you really didn't know the person's real name until they died. That is when you find out the person's real name. I always thought that was very sad, so I said if I ever have a baby, I would never use a nickname either.

My mom and dad both had twins run in their families. Her mom's side of the family had identical twin girls and another family member had two sets of twins. My dad had twin sisters. I was happy to see these two new beautiful babies. They were so small at the time, but we were crazy about them. I knew that I would have to help my mother with the twins; I knew I would have to do things like getting the bottles of milk warm, changing their diapers, feeding them, and helping with babysitting. I even had to get up in the middle of the night to warm their milk especially when it was cold at night. I also knew that I would have to help out a lot around the house when Dad would leave for work offshore. With Dad working

Wounds
For Love Comes Tragic and Painful

offshore, that meant helping Mom out more around the house.

With the new babies at home, I remember we loved to hold the babies. I just loved the way the babies smelled, how they made these funny faces while they were sleeping, and when I made them smile or laugh. I enjoyed spoiling them to death. I remember when the twins were three months old, my parents had gone to visit at one of my aunt's and uncle's. They left me to babysit my siblings and the twins. I was in the kitchen finishing up with some dishes when I heard the twins crying in my parents' bedroom.

I asked my oldest sister under me, Carla, to go get the twins, but she was scared of the dark so she didn't want to go get them. I asked one of the other kids, but no one wanted to get the babies. I couldn't believe that my sisters were so afraid of the dark that they wouldn't get the babies. I decided that I would go get the twins, and on my way back I had each of the twins – one in each arm. As I walked down the hall back to the living room with the twins in my arms, when I got to the hall door, my other sister, Sara, came from behind me and stepped on the back of my slipper by accident. I fell straight down on my knees with the babies still in my arms. As I tried to get up

-Growing Up-

with the twins still in my arms, the babies wouldn't stop crying. I didn't think the babies were hurt too badly because when I fell, they were still in my arms. During the fall, I was not aware that one of the twin's legs had hit the wall in the doorway.

Shortly afterwards, my parents came home. I told them what happened, and I was so scared because I didn't know what my parents were going to do. I remembered my parents taking the kids to my Aunt Helen and Uncle Andrew's while they took the babies to the hospital to find out what was wrong with the babies when they wouldn't stop crying. I knew something was wrong when my dad came back with one of the twins. I heard him tell my aunt and uncle that the other twin's leg was broken. My mom was still at the hospital with my little baby sister, while the doctor was putting a cast on her leg. When we got home, it wasn't until days later that my mom told me and my siblings the story of what happen at the hospital. My mom told us that the doctor kept pulling and pulling on my sister's leg, and she kept crying and crying. My mom then said she screamed at the doctor to stop pulling her baby's leg. The twins were only three months old at the time, and my mom kept expressing how here she is only three months old with a cast on her leg. Mom was very angry. Time went by and nothing more happened, and I thought everything was fine. Months later my sister's leg

WOUNDS
FOR LOVE COMES TRAGIC AND PAINFUL

began to heal, and I remember thanking God that now my sister's leg is healing. I was thinking Dad and Mom had forgotten about the incident. But one day my other sisters had been acting up. Anyone who has younger siblings know that they can be a pain in the butt sometimes; they can get you into trouble – even without trying. That was the day I and my siblings got our asses whipped like never before. That day, even though it was months later, my ass whipping was about the twin's leg that had gotten broken.

    I felt like I shouldn't have gotten my ass whipped for that, but my mom said it was because we lied about it. I didn't remember lying at all about what happened; I told the truth! I felt my sister, Sara, should have been punished for stepping on the back of my slipper. It had always been my brother and sisters who were too afraid to tell my parents the truth about things that happened – not me. When they knew I was going to tell my parents what they did when we were home alone, they would gang up on me and put all the blame on me. As a teenager growing up, I hated when I had to babysit my brother and sisters because they were always getting into some kind of trouble or problem when my parents were away and I would get punished for it. After that incident with the twins, I was always nervous about having to stay home with my siblings while my parents were away. Since then, my sisters and brother did have other accidents. There was the time my sister, Sara got cut on the back of her leg from the chain on her bicycle, and also the time my brother got hit by a car while riding his bicycle on the road one Saturday afternoon. I remember being glad that their accidents weren't more serious than what they were, and that my family was home at the time, because that meant I couldn't get blamed for them.

THE OLD COUNTRY ROAD

As I remembered more and more from my childhood, I discovered that I had a treasure chest filled with memories that I had kept hidden for so long. As that treasure chest continued to open up, I was surprised to find that as a child I had more good memories than bad. I remembered growing up in our old house – the one house I remembered the most. There were so many good memories I could cherish like the time I got my first period, my first kiss, first boyfriend, first house party, our family's first Christmas party, and like I said, when the twins were born.

I also remembered the time when my dad was teaching me and my brother how to drive. It was much easier back then to learn to drive because we lived in the country and we didn't have to worry about traffic. We had two vehicles at the time, a

WOUNDS
FOR LOVE COMES TRAGIC AND PAINFUL

Crown Victoria and a green Ford pickup. One Saturday or Sunday evening, we were on our way home from visiting my aunt and uncle. I remember on that day me and my sisters were riding in the car with Mom, and my dad and brother, Jay, were riding in the truck. On the way home, my dad and Jay were right behind us, but we made it home first before them. My mom started wondering what was taking them so long to get home. When Mom stepped outside, she could see that cars were stopping in this big curve that was not far from our home. She jumped in the car and we all got in with her to see what the matter was. It was my dad and Jay! Dad was teaching Jay how to drive when they had a blowout and the truck had flipped upside down in the ditch going in the other direction. It was so scary to pull up and see that! I was just glad that my dad and brother weren't killed or hurt. They were blessed to be alive! I remember Dad took full responsibility for the accident which could have happened to anyone.

Those country roads were nothing to be played with. We lived way out in the country so we had to be careful whenever we were going somewhere like going to church all the time. There was a long country dirt road that took us to church every week. You can imagine when it rained how slippery muddy it was at times, or when it was a very windy day and the roads were very dusty so that you couldn't see very well.

-Growing Up-

The roads were dusty and the cars were too. Yes, I even remembered the road. Every curve, ditch, and bump in that old country road was important to me.

    I especially remembered riding on that road the first day and time I worked in a potato field. When I was out of school during the summer, I would work in the fields sometime to make extra money to help out with getting my school supplies. I recall one time when both my brother and I wanted to go into the fields to work with the adults in the family that day, but they only had room for one more person in the truck. My parents said that I could go. I looked at my brother Jay's face and saw that he was upset because he wanted to go so badly. For some reason, I felt relieved that my mom didn't let my brother go even though I felt sad when I looked at Jay's face.

    Later on that day, I was thankful that it was me who was chosen to go because that was the day my Uncle Henry had the blowout on his truck, killing two people and injuring several others. I was a passenger in the truck and all I remember is waking up seated on a pallet with lots of nails all scratched up. One of my cousins was killed in that blowout and another lady was too. That was one of the saddest days I recall because my cousin, Caroline, was

Wounds
For Love Comes Tragic and Painful

planning a wedding; she was to be married that same year.

    The first thing I thought of was how glad I was that my brother couldn't come because he could have been one of those killed or severely injured. I thanked God that my mom had picked me and didn't let my brother go that day. Being the oldest, I had always felt responsible for my siblings. I knew that Mom believed in praying and going to church and we were in church every Sunday, sometime all day. I believe that is what saved me and my brother that day, my Mom's prayers and wisdom.

Virgin Bride

I found myself remembering all about my childhood – the good and the bad. I learned I had a great childhood. It was becoming an adult that endangered my memory. As I thought about my teenage years, I remembered wanting to grow up fast as a child. I wished now that I had waited and prolonged getting married as long as I could. I could have learned some things about life, like how to love myself first, and how to handle validating myself even when those I loved couldn't love me back. If I had waited longer to get married maybe I could have learned how not to worry so much about boys.

I met a boy at church or I should say, young man. He was four years older than I was and already out of school working for a living. He was tall, handsome, hardworking, and into church – the kind of boy that every young girl dreamed of dating. I remember when I started dating him, we were living in that same house where most of my childhood memories took place. He was my first boyfriend and I recall being so nervous when he came over for the first time. I also noticed that my siblings would always peep around the corner looking into the living room to see what we were doing.

WOUNDS
FOR LOVE COMES TRAGIC AND PAINFUL

His name was Adam and he was an usher at the church where our choir had to sing that afternoon. I remember him asking me if he could call me sometime, and I knew that he would have to call and ask my parents first if he could come over. I thought for sure they would say no, but they told him only on the weekends. When he came over the first time, my parents had a long talk with him about the rules. Dad told Adam he could see me only on weekends, not on weeknights. Adam was able to see me on Friday evenings though Sunday until ten o'clock which was fine because Adam worked on weekdays.

He sported a Jerri-curl hairstyle and that was popular in the late 70's and early 80's. People were proud of their curls back then. Of course when he came over to see me, all eyes were on him. We had no privacy at all. The siblings were always looking around the corner to see what we were doing.

I was glad that Adam was also raised in the church because I always wanted a man that was about God's business. I liked the fact that he was a hard worker also. When we met, he was working for a tree nursery, a company that planted and grew trees and other kinds of plants.

- Virgin Bride -

Nearly three years later, we moved across town and Adam and I were still dating. But now, he had to drive much farther to see me. Since Adam worked for a tree company, he had given my dad beautiful trees to plant in the front and back yard of our new house.

I recall it was not long after we had been living in the new home, when I was finishing up with the dishes one night and getting ready to mop the floor, Mom came right out and blurted the age-old question – *"When was your last period?"* Everyone had gone to bed except my brother. He was watching television, and right in front of him, my mom just came right out and blurted that question. Prior to that, my parents had been in their bedroom, but now Mom, moving like a freight train, made her way into the kitchen, just to hit me with that question. I was very stunned by that, and embarrassed too because my brother was seated right there in front of us.

I told my mother that it had been about two months and I continued to mop the floor. Immediately Mom goes back into her bedroom and comes back out to tell me Dad wanted to see me. When I stepped into their room, I was shocked as Dad started asking me more questions about my period! Now I was flabbergasted – even more having

Wounds
For Love Comes Tragic and Painful

to talk with Dad about such female things, especially since my mother and I never had such talks!

I couldn't believe it. All these years had gone by and we had no talk about sex, periods, babies, or boys. Now, all of sudden, it's after-dinner talk time about sex! At the time I couldn't understand what the big deal was. Mom barely talked to me about her period or anything else for that matter, much less sex! I was happy when I hadn't seen my period for months because I hated when it was that time of the month. I recall my dad asking me if I was having sex. I was shocked and I told my parents that I wasn't having any sex. That night, I wasn't sure what my parents were talking about, but I went back into the kitchen to finish mopping the floor before going to bed.

The next thing I knew, my mom had made an appointment for me to see the doctor. She said it was to find out if I was pregnant. At the time, I was confused about all this. The doctor came back with test results telling my mom that I wasn't pregnant. But then it still wasn't over; my mom now had to take me somewhere to be treated for my female cycle problems. At the time, I felt like I had done something wrong and got female problems. It felt like my parents didn't believe me, and I was being shoved from one doctor to another. I knew that me and my boyfriend had fooled around a little hugged up with each other with all our clothes on, but that was it. I was so scared to death of what might happen to me; I never thought about getting pregnant or doing anything more than kissing and touching. My parents now had me so confused that I didn't know if I was pregnant or not! I started thinking I could get pregnant by kissing and touching. I was still a virgin, but after my parents took me here and there making me scared, I started to believe that maybe I could have gotten pregnant like that. I was puzzled by the fact that my parents thought that I was having sex just because I didn't have a period for a couple months. I was just that naïve and untrained.

Back then things were very different. My parents didn't talk about sex and subjects like pregnancy, so I didn't really know how to get pregnant! But I knew I hadn't been naked with anyone or had sex. Besides, all through high school the guys had never approached me like that. They were not interested in me. When they did approach me, it was to tease me or mess with me because of my mean-talking and bossy ways. There might have been some guys that were interested in me, but they never said anything to me about it. I was very head-strong at the time, feisty, and outspoken like my mom's mother, Mamáu Amy. When it came to guys or men, I wasn't going to have them or no one challenge me.

WOUNDS
FOR LOVE COMES TRAGIC AND PAINFUL

I took that after my dad's family ways, too. My relatives were always very abrupt with their words. It was the way we communicated; we were not mean, that was just the way our French Cajun Creole dialect came out. I learned over the years that people thought I had a mean abrupt manner of speaking and communicating with them. At school, they said I sounded sharp when I talked and others as I got older told me the same thing. I remember thinking to myself that it didn't feel good hearing people tell me something was wrong with the way that I talked. Then, one day I caught myself being harsh with my words. It wasn't a very good feeling when I heard myself talking. I couldn't believe how I sounded. I made a promise to myself that I was going to change that and work on that area of my life. I was always striving for perfection. Though things were not easy, I would always keep on trying until I would get it right. I was so used to hearing my family speak that way when I grew up, that I learned to speak sharply and fast. I didn't see anything wrong with how we communicated. But when I was out on my own, that is when I realized that people were offended by the way I spoke to them, so I would work on that from time to time. As far as communicating with Adam, he and I never had a problem communicating or understanding one another. I did notice at times, he would get a little jealous when we were dating, but we never had a problem talking things over between us.

THE PERFECT WEDDING

Adam and I had been dating for nearly three years when he asked me to marry him, and I said yes. I knew that Adam had to talk to my parents first to get their approval. After all, he was four years older than me and I was still in school. In all our years of dating, nothing unusual ever happened. He always followed my dad's rules and was extremely courteous to me and others.

Adam was a very shy and reserved person; he was always a very hard working man. He was a gentleman – always opening the door for me and speaking nicely to me. He did things to show me that he was sweet, kind, romantic, and he loved helping others in need. He had a truck and a motor cycle and I loved to see him smile. I saw that smile a lot when he would ride his motorcycle. I believe he felt free while riding on that wide open country road that we lived on. A church-going man, I knew that he didn't drink, smoke, or party. I liked that about him. We both loved going to church.

I had no reservations about saying yes when Adam finally asked me to marry him after nearly three years of us dating. We were engaged around Christmas 1979. We set the date for June 14, 1980.

WOUNDS
FOR LOVE COMES TRAGIC AND PAINFUL

Mom had to tell me not to set my wedding date on the week of my period! I thought, *"Huh?!"* It was hard enough because I had irregular cycles. Even after going to the doctor's that time, my period never came on the same week or the same day of the month like normal girls. I thought that's life for you. I go all these years without talking about sex or hardly anything with my mom, and now that I'm getting married, that's all we're talking about – sex! But when she did start talking to me about it, I listened! I believed in so many ways that was what made my mom, Glory Jean, so special. Here she was, lovingly, trying to tell me about my dues as a wife. I understood what my mom was explaining to me about sex, and I respected her for trying to give me a heads up. This was all new to me. Just my luck - I thought my period might come during the week of our wedding, and guess what, it did! But I managed to dodge a bullet! The day of our wedding was the last day of my menstrual cycle! The flow had already stopped, and I was so happy, and scared all at the same time.

    I remember getting everything ready for our wedding day. There was so much to be done! I chose a rainbow theme and my mom and I went looking for wedding dresses. I tried on so many wedding dresses until I found the right one that wasn't too expensive. I was so in love back then. I wanted a nice size wedding, so I had seven girls and seven boys in the wedding party. Things were going so well for us.

Adam was also making sure that he had everything for our wedding. He found a house out in Grand Prairie, Louisiana, not far from where his parents lived before they got married. He took me to see the house before our marriage. It was a two bedroom house which was just perfect for us. My parents bought us a bedroom set and a dining room set as a wedding gift. I knew that my parents would be very generous with helping us get everything we needed for the new house. That was the most beautiful thing that they had ever done for me. My fiancé, Adam, bought a bedroom set for our master bedroom, a living room set, and all of the appliances for the new house.

There was one thing that happened that made me very disappointed around this time. Adam's parents - they seemed happy that their son was getting married, but then when it came down to the last couple of days, his parents decided they were not coming to the wedding. I don't know why this happened, but I knew that it was very hurtful for Adam that his parents were not going to come. I felt his pain, and I was also sad myself that they weren't going to come to our wedding. I knew Adam was very

WOUNDS
FOR LOVE COMES TRAGIC AND PAINFUL

devastated about them not coming. I had all my family there and there were others in his family, but we wanted his parents to be there also to share in the celebration.

I was so happy that both my grandparents were going to be there. I was their oldest granddaughter and the first to get married. Even though I had been told that other members of his family were going to be there, I knew there was nothing like having your own parents there too to wish you well in your marriage. Adam's parents were very strict and disciplined more than my parents did at the time.

I was told in the past that his father was a very mean and hateful man, extremely overprotective of his children. I was surprised that Adam's father wouldn't let his children or his wife come to the wedding. He knew that his daughter was in the wedding and even she couldn't come. All of this didn't make sense to me then. His children were grown and some of his sons and daughters were older than I was. I was hurt by the fact that Adam's sisters and his mom wanted to come to the wedding, but his dad wouldn't allow them to. Folks had said that he was a very controlling man who believed in working his children to death. I was also told later on after we were married that his dad was into witchcraft or some might call it voodoo.

Witchcraft had been around for centuries back then. A lot of folk were off into witchcraft and I believe many people still are till this day, but not everyone from Louisiana is into that stuff. Some people from Louisiana know very little to nothing about witchcraft. Just because one is from Louisiana doesn't mean one is about witchcraft! Not so!

Adam's dad had a lot of rules for him and his siblings. They were all grown, but still living with his parents. Folks said it was because he loved being in control of his children and his wife. They weren't allowed to go anywhere unless he said so. They had no life. I noticed the only place they were allowed to go was to church and the grocery store, and he was there with them the whole time.

Adam had an older brother who was already married, and it was said his older sister had left home because of her dad being very over-protective. It was said that she wasn't allowed to date anyone, and she was in her late twenties at the time. I was told that she left home and never came back.

Wounds
For Love Comes Tragic and Painful

Our wedding day finally came! My dad, who I was so proud of, walked me down the aisle in my beautiful long white wedding dress. My wedding day was beautiful! We had a beautiful wedding reception at the church. At our reception, I knew that there would be lots of alcohol and I knew that some of my family members loved to drink while others in the family would only have a drink or two. Adam and I were not ones to drink, but I thought that for our wedding day we might have a taste of wine for when we made a toast to our marriage.

When it was time for the toast, I took a sip of my wine, but Adam wouldn't even have a taste. I didn't see anything wrong with a taste of wine on our wedding day. But Adam wouldn't have anything to do with it, so I was okay with that. The reception continued and everyone had a good time.

I had a big family and they had showered me with so many beautiful gifts. My husband and I didn't have to worry about buying anything for our new home. Everything had been set up in our new home before we got married, so all we had to do was come home after our wedding reception was over and enjoy our honeymoon.

- VIRGIN BRIDE -

The wedding reception was now coming to an end. My family was wrapping things up, and we were on our way to our honeymoon. I remember being so scared and nervous because at the time I was still a virgin. We had never had sex while we were dating – in all those three years!

Over the years growing up, I had heard girls talk about their first experience at school. Some were good and some were bad. I wasn't sure what to believe. The time had finally come and I was looking forward to a new beginning, and a wonderful experience that I had been waiting for my whole life – the experience of sharing myself with my new husband! I had dreamed of this day for a long time. I had imagined what it would be like to share this wonderful experience with my husband. I not only wanted everything to be special, but perfect and romantic for the both of us.

Although I was nervous and scared, I knew that this would be a wonderful night for me and my husband, Adam, to take our love to the next level. What made it even more special is that we were both virgins, and this was in the eighties! Remarkable, I thought! I believed when two people are in love like we were, sharing a bond between the two of us sealing our love for each other would be a beautiful thing.

WOUNDS
FOR LOVE COMES TRAGIC AND PAINFUL

Adam was my soul mate and we were going to share a lifetime of experience together - the good and the bad.

We planned to spend our honeymoon in our new home. It was perfect! I liked living in the country. That's why I was so happy that we found a house way out. The country houses were far apart, and once we got a phone, it would be great. As Adam was driving us home on our way to our honeymoon, I noticed that he kept talking about the fact that I had a taste of wine. I couldn't believe the way he was starting to make a big deal out of me having wine when everyone was toasting at our wedding reception. I was well aware that both of us didn't drink, but I didn't see anything wrong with having a taste of wine on my wedding day during the toast to each other. I felt that it would help relax me for my wedding night. I knew that I wasn't the only woman out there who had ever been nervous on her wedding night, not to mention experiencing sex for the first time! The fact that I was about to lose my virginity after all these years of waiting while dating my first love made my stomach nervous. I felt being a virgin was the easy part; it was when I had to leap over to the other side that made me scared - not knowing what to expect or how I would feel after the sex part was over. But I was ready for the challenge because I loved Adam so much! He was my soul mate!

Let He who is Without Sin

In the car, I felt that my new husband was looking for an argument, and I unfortunately had given him one by taking our wedding toast. I was afraid that I had spoiled our honeymoon; I wasn't sure what the problem was. I thought maybe he was just as nervous, or maybe he was scared as I was at the time; I thought perhaps he didn't know how to tell me. I knew that women were different from men when it came to expressing their feelings. I was well aware that men didn't express their feelings like women do; they have a way of hiding their feelings and their love.

We finally made it to our new home to celebrate our honeymoon. I recalled Adam carried me into the house. I remembered after he carried me into the house, I was so tired, but so excited at the same time. I wanted to get out of my wedding dress, and slip into something a little sexier for him. So I went into the restroom to change, and he was in the living room. Although I was so scared and nervous, I knew the time had finally come, and I couldn't turn back now. I delicately stepped out of the room all beautiful and glowing. With a shy smile looking at my husband in the living room, I couldn't help but imagine what

Wounds
For Love Comes Tragic and Painful

his words would be from seeing me in my carefully chosen honeymoon lingerie - seeing me in it for the first time intimately. To my shock and dismay, what happened next was not at all what I expected. Adam started arguing, accusing me of not being a virgin and talking very badly to me.

I couldn't believe it! All this time I waited and dreamed about. Never in a million years did I imagine my honeymoon night would be like this. I came out dressed for him in this sexy lingerie on what was to be our special night to remember, and this was the gift I had waited for? I asked him, *"Why would you say something like that knowing it wasn't true?"* I noticed that my husband was finding all kinds of excuses to continue this fight. I had no idea what was up with him. I was thinking, *"This is our wedding night; we are supposed to be the happiest people in the world right now. Yet, we are a new couple arguing over our wedding toast and whether or not I am a virgin? Come on, is he serious?"*

I thought for a moment, *"Oh wow, we hadn't made love yet. What was he basing this on? I thought that both of us were virgins!"* I knew that he was older than me, so I asked him if he was still a virgin, and he got mad at me for asking that question. After that, he decided he didn't want to talk anymore, so he sat in the living room watching television while I was trying to understand what just happened. In the meantime, I started getting ready for bed hoping he would come in once I got into bed. I remembered asking him to come to bed. He said that he would be there in fifteen minutes. So I waited and waited for him until finally, I fell asleep.

I was awakened by the sound of something ripping apart very loudly as the bed covers were quickly snatched off of me. It was my husband, tearing my lingerie with a hunting knife. He then jumped on top of me with his hunting knife in one hand, and his other hand over my mouth telling me to keep my mouth shut, and not to scream. I had no idea what he was doing as he then took his hand off my mouth with the knife still in his other hand. Then he raped me with the knife to my throat. While he was on top of me raping me like he was some kind of savage animal, he told me if I said anything to anyone about this, he would kill me. For some reason, I knew by looking at him with this knife to my head that he wasn't joking. I felt that my life was in danger, and I didn't know what to do.

I was in shock at what just happened to me. All I could do was lay there crying with tears rolling down my face. I remember feeling sorry, hurt, and numb – not to mention I was in pain when he was

WOUNDS
FOR LOVE COMES TRAGIC AND PAINFUL

finished. I thought that he had raped me like that because he didn't believe that I was a virgin. Then after he was finished, he went back into the living room and watched television like nothing happened. No one can ever imagine what that was like for me. As I continued to lie in bed hurting, bleeding, and confused, I felt my heart drop to the floor. I was wondering, *"What have I done?"*

Later on that night, when he decided to come to bed, he started talking to me and wanted to apologize. At the time, I wasn't feeling like hearing what he had to say. So that night, I was so horrified and upset that all I could do was cry my heart out confused and hurt. Afterwards, I just cried myself to sleep. The next morning was a Sunday morning and before going to church he wanted to make love to me. He said he wanted to make up for the night before. He started talking nicely to me. He said something about not wanting to ruin our wedding night, and he didn't even explain why he had done what he did.

Adam knew I was a sucker for love and romance. I even believed in true love; that is how naïve I was back then. I had no idea what I was in for. I believed intimacy was a beautiful thing, and that it played a big part in a relationship when a person is in love with their soul mate. All kinds of feelings were running through my head. It was the next day after the wedding; I thought that we would stay home, after all, it was our honeymoon. But he wanted me to go with him to his church that morning. I wanted to stay home. Adam really wanted me to go to church with him so I agreed to go.

After church, on our way home, Adam started complaining about me turning my head toward the back door of the church. He wanted to know who I was looking for. I told him that I wasn't looking for anyone. I said that it was a reflex that I do that all the time. I explained that it wasn't the first time he had seen me do that, and I didn't see what the big deal was. Besides, I explained, *"Since you are an usher at the back door, I was looking at my tall handsome man standing at the back door."* I told him that I always turned my head to see who came into the church; it was just a habit, and I kept trying to explain that I wasn't the only one who had been looking at the back door of the church a time or two.

I remember that Sunday while driving home after church, Adam just wouldn't let it go; he kept complaining, and I realized that he had gotten angry and upset. When we arrived home, I went into the bedroom to change my clothes before cooking dinner. Adam entered the bedroom to change his clothes as

WOUNDS
FOR LOVE COMES TRAGIC AND PAINFUL

well, but when he did that, I didn't realize that he was going to beat me again. This time it was for turning my head around in church. From out of nowhere, as I was changing my clothes, he sucker-punched me so hard in my stomach that I didn't even see it coming. All I could do was fall down to the floor. Then he just kept beating and kicking me. I was trying to protect myself when he was kicking me, but I couldn't move. He had me pinned in a corner. I kept asking him to stop. I was crying and hurting. Finally, when he was through beating and kicking me as I was on the floor, he then pulled me up, and with the same hunting knife to my throat, he dared me to tell anyone about this.

Adam then went into the living room to watch television, and he demanded me to hurry up with cooking his dinner. When I finished cooking, I had to fix his food and bring his plate of food with a glass of water to him. When he was finished, I had to get his plate and bring it to the kitchen to wash. I remember thinking I didn't have a problem with cooking and fixing his food. I didn't mind waiting on him and serving him. I had learned from watching my mom and the other women in my family over the years. They would pamper their husbands. I was accustomed to seeing the women in my family wait on their husbands; they would fix their husband's food and bring it to them. I was prepared for that. But

-Let He who is Without Sin-

I was not prepared for getting my ass beat. I thought he was treating me like I was a piece of trash.

After dinner Adam went back to watching the television show or his sports, whichever it was, while I was finishing up in the kitchen. I was very upset and afraid of my husband's attitude and his temper, not to mention his violent rage. When I was finished washing the dishes, Adam demanded me to put on something sexy to model for him. I noticed very quickly that he was being very controlling. That was another side of him that I had never seen before in him. Before I knew anything, Adam was saying that he was sorry again. I thought by the look and the expression on his face that he was sorry for what he had done to me, but I felt that didn't excuse him from hurting me. He was trying to make it up to me, but by then, I was so scared of him that I didn't know what to expect at that point.

I remember trying to put it out of my mind, but he began to beg me for forgiveness, I was so unsure of myself and what I was doing in this kind of situation that I did forgive him. I thought it was just some kind of mistake and that he was just having problems adjusting to marriage. I really thought that he loved me and I loved him, and that this was what I was supposed to do in order to make our relationship

WOUNDS
FOR LOVE COMES TRAGIC AND PAINFUL

a marriage – a commitment to one another. He kissed me so he could get me in the mood. At that point, he was moving his attention away from the television and trying to be intimate with me. I was a little surprised when he wanted to be intimate with me during his sports time. This made me feel like he really did want to be nice to me. I recall my husband telling me to give him fifteen or twenty minutes, and for me to go ahead to bed and he would be there shortly. So because I was struggling to believe that this man really did want me, I decided to forgive him and try to turn things around. I went in the bedroom ahead of him to make sure everything was perfect for when Adam would come to bed. Everything was so crazy; I remember thinking, *"After all, we are still on our honeymoon."* I remember lighting the candle in the bedroom so that it would be a little more romantic. I felt like maybe there was something I could do to help him. So I slipped into sexy lingerie just for Adam. When he came to bed, he was very intimate with me that night. It was the first time he had been intimate and not a savage with me.

It was now Monday morning and my husband had to go to work that morning, and everything was ok between us. I recall trying to make sure that my husband had something to eat when he came home for lunch that day. Adam had told me that he would be home for lunchtime and I wanted to make sure he had something to eat. At that time I didn't have much to do around the house other than straighten up. Being a newlywed, I thought I would later try to find a job. I wanted to make sure my husband's dinner was ready when he came home from work. I wanted to make sure everything was perfect for him. I knew my husband was a very hard working man and he worked outdoors, so I wanted to make sure that all he had to do when he came home from work was to relax. I even had his bath water ready for him when he came home. Things were very different in those times than they are now with women. I know that in today's society, most women wouldn't have done a lot of things that I did as a wife. I didn't mind doing whatever it took to make my husband happy. I knew he worked outside in the heat and I knew what that could do to a person.

Well one night I tried to have his bath water hot and ready for him when he came home. There were times when I wasn't sure what time he got off work because there were days he would work late, and during that time we had no phone for him to call home. I recall one day I wasn't feeling good and my husband had worked late, so when he came home his bath water had gotten cold by the time he got in from work. Because I wasn't feeling well on that day, I also didn't have his dinner ready for him. Adam wanted to know why his dinner wasn't ready. I remember

WOUNDS
FOR LOVE COMES TRAGIC AND PAINFUL

telling him that I wasn't feeling good. That didn't matter to him. Not only was he mad because his dinner wasn't ready, but he was also mad when his bath had gotten cold. I had to add more hot water, which I felt he could have done himself. I didn't like it when he got upset because there was no telling what he would do to me as punishment. I recall thinking to myself saying, "Oh wow, what's up with all the complaining on every little thing." I couldn't believe how he was finding things to complain about. I also noticed quickly in our marriage that everything had to be perfect for him, or I would have to pay the price later when he decided he wanted to beat me or threaten to kill me. I felt that was not a way for me to live. Not knowing when my husband's attitude or his bad day would go up in a rage of violence, I wasn't sure how much I could take.

Adam loved watching television, and he would stay up late, so I would watch television with him until it was time for bed. I didn't like it when he stayed up too late. At times, he would wait until I was fast asleep, and then he would pull some kind of stunt. When I did go into the bedroom, I sometimes would find myself falling asleep before he came in to bed. At times, I never knew when he would try something crazy when I was asleep, like pulling the cover off of me very quickly with his hunting knife ripping or cutting my night gown and my panties right off. He would also put his knife to my throat and then rape me like he was some kind of animal. That became his pattern. At the time, I begin to feel like maybe he was possessed; I just couldn't understand what would make him do those things to me. When he would finish raping me and threatening me, he would then tell me if I told anyone he would kill me.

At first, I wasn't sure if he was serious or bluffing about killing me at the time. I was too scared to challenge him or give him an ultimatum. For the first time in my life, I felt weak, not knowing what to do about it. Usually, I was a pretty outspoken person, but now I found myself seriously puzzled and scared for my life all at the same time, and still in love with the person I knew before we were married.

It wasn't like I could talk to anyone other than my parents, and he was always seated there with me so I couldn't tell my parents what was going on at the time. The very next day he was always sorry for what he had done to me, and again my husband would beg me to forgive him. Sometimes, I felt like maybe he wasn't sorry for what he did; maybe he was just using sympathy as a poor excuse. He not only knew that he had hurt me, but he also knew that I was very angry with him. There were times when Adam would try to

WOUNDS
FOR LOVE COMES TRAGIC AND PAINFUL

make it up to me, and because I was scared of him, I would give in and let him make it up to me. That would always last until the next time he would do something to pull his stunts again. He would always jump down my throat when I came home and his dinner wasn't ready quick enough or his bath water wasn't hot enough. My evening routine was to fix his food and bring it to him after he was done with his bath. After that, I would then clean up the kitchen. When I was finished, I would proceed to our bedroom to get myself ready for bed since my husband was always watching television. There were times when my husband would enter into our bedroom as I was getting ready for bed. Then he would grab me and push me up against the dresser and start beating me because I didn't have his dinner ready when he got home from work. I would try to defend myself by fighting back, but I was only making things worse because then he would hit me much harder. He always had that knife to my throat threatening to kill me when he would beat and rape me. He beat me so badly that I could barely get up. My stomach, ribs, arms, legs and head were hurting and in pain. He always made sure he hit me where no one could see the bruises on my body. Adam made sure when he beat me that he didn't hit me in the face, so no one could see.

-LET HE WHO IS WITHOUT SIN -

I didn't realize what kind of man I had married. I had no idea that he was an abusive man. When he would rape and beat me and then apologize, he would always give me that pitiful look in his eyes like he was sorry. He even at times would cry like a baby with real tears in his eyes as if he was sincerely sorry for hurting me. I remember seeing this and begging my husband to stop beating and threatening to kill me. I thought if he did listen to me and stop it then, maybe I would know that he was sincere with his apologies. But I came to not trust his words for one minute. I remember thinking that if I could just get a hold of the knife from under his pillow at night, I would feel better. But he had guarded that knife with his life, and it was never out of his sight. I recall feeling helpless, lost, scared, and confused, but somehow I was going to figure out how to get the knife from him while he was sleeping. Lying in our bed thinking to myself how I was going to get out from under him, I felt like maybe he really was going to kill me one day.

I was too afraid to tell my parents without my husband knowing about it and not knowing what he might do. I didn't understand the reason behind all this considering that we were newlyweds. I recall thinking, *"We shouldn't have any problems; we have only been married for a couple of weeks."* I remember telling myself, *"If this is how things are going to be between us,*

WOUNDS
FOR LOVE COMES TRAGIC AND PAINFUL

then I don't know if I can live like this." I recall getting an attitude when my parents used to whip me as a child, and I certainly wasn't prepared for a man or my husband to beat me. I wasn't the same anymore after my husband had beat and rape me. My attitude was starting to change toward my husband. I was having a hard time accepting the fact that this was the same man in that short time of our marriage. I began to wonder what else this man was hiding from me since before we were married. I had heard that his dad was a very mean man, and I figured he might have had something to do with my husband being abusive. I had heard that nine out of ten times when children are raised in abusive homes, they become very abusive themselves. I thought, whatever the case may be love can be blind, but not that blind. I didn't believe in falling into the wrong kind of love, but yet I was being told by my husband repeatedly that he would kill me and burn me ten feet underground where no one could ever find my body. I was beside myself to hear this, being in love with my husband. I couldn't understand where this was all coming from, and I wasn't sure what I was going to do about it.

I told my husband that I wanted him to make love to me, not rape me. I tried explaining to him that this was supposed to be a very special time for both of us, and again he would say that he was sorry. My mind and my heart were shattered to pieces having been taken by him like that, with his choosing to savagely rape me instead of making passionate love to me in an experience both of us would enjoy. I was so confused; I was in a state of denial even though this had happened to me. I couldn't believe that this was what I had waited for all my life. I thought, *"How stupid was I that I had let this happen to me."*

In the first few weeks after our marriage when we had gone to my parent's house, I was not able to tell my parents. I would always pretend in front of my parents like everything was okay. I knew my parents weren't crazy. They knew something was wrong; Mom could always tell when something was wrong with anyone of her children. I had been thinking of leaving him although we were still newlyweds. But my husband was always sorry for his actions afterward and when he thought that I wasn't buying it, he would threaten to kill me. Although I wanted to leave him, at the same time, I was also ashamed and embarrassed about what other people would say about me. My husband loved throwing a guilt trip on me about what other people might think, and then he would scare me by telling me how he would be killing me if I talked about leaving him. He would always say, *"I'll bury your body where no one could find you, not even your family."* I never knew that someone could be that mean and evil to a person, especially someone who'd just gotten married. I kept

Wounds
For Love Comes Tragic and Painful

letting the thoughts of marriage and the sacredness of it keep getting in the way of me making a right decision. He had gotten to the point where he was not only violent and jealous, but also manipulative. I couldn't stand him lying about how sorry he was after he beat me up; I hated giving in to his sorry excuses, but at the same time, I felt weak and helpless at that point. I was thinking about how much I loved my husband and how this had taken a toll on our marriage. This man was my first love and I couldn't get over it. I remembered him being a true gentleman when we were dating. He seemed to always consider my feelings then. I remembered how he used to take me for rides on his motorcycle, or drive us to the park in his truck, or take me to the movies, or sometimes we just went out for a drive in the country. I recall he would even take my sisters sometimes when he came to visit me on the weekends when we were dating. We both had spent so much time at church on the weekends together. My parents had even grown to like him as part of the family. We used to cuddle up in the living room of my parents house together every weekend. Although we dated for almost three years, not once did I see any sign of abuse. I did notice however at times that he was a little jealous, but I thought what man wasn't jealous at some time or another. I felt that everyone has some form of jealousy in them, but it's how they handle it that matters. I thought, *"Even my dad is a little jealous, but he never put his hand on my mom or abused her."*

For the first time in my life, I started thinking about how dangerous life can be in the country with no phone or anyone to help me when my husband would abuse me. I had enjoyed living in the country with my parents, and I had no idea living in the country with my husband would be different. We had no phone and houses were so far apart back, I recall. There was also not much street light except for the lights on the cars and trucks that passed by. I recall asking my husband to get a phone put in the house for emergencies, and he quickly told me, "No!" His excuse was if he put a phone in the house, I would be on it all the time. But I knew the real reason why he didn't want one. Adam knew if we had a phone I would have called the police or my parents and he didn't want that. Too many times there were days when he came home from work and he was in a bad mood. When he had a rough day at work, I knew I would have to fasten my seat belt; it would be a bumpy ride for me that day. There were times when things were good between us. He would cuddle up with me on the sofa while watching television, talking, laughing or telling some kind of jokes to each other. He was a good man as long as he wasn't being abusive, controlling, arrogant, or manipulative, being sorry for hurting me. That was the other side of him.

WOUNDS
FOR LOVE COMES TRAGIC AND PAINFUL

Adam knew I didn't like to fight, but there were times just out of the blue when he loved catching me off guard when I was going into our bedroom to do something. He made it a habit of using me as a punching bag, like I was a man. I would try to defend myself, but every time I did, he would hit me much harder. I could never win with him. I was a strong woman I thought, but not strong enough to fight my husband off.

When I was raped, I never considered myself a victim because I thought of him as my husband, even when he would beat the scrap out of me and threaten to kill me all the time. He would sometimes beat me so badly that I was not able to move at all. I had to just lie there for a while until the pain would ease up. My biggest fear was when he would threaten me with his knife and tell me that he would bury me where no one would find me. I felt that I could take the beating but not him threatening to kill me. That was a big pill to swallow. I just knew one day my husband would snap and when he did, he would kill me. All I wanted was to deal with this and get out before it was too late, but he always made it hard for me to leave. He loved pulling the covers off of me very quickly when I had gone to bed, and jumping on top of me with that knife in his hand up to my throat like I was some kind of animal. I remember crying many nights before finally going to sleep after he'd rape or beat me. I was upset with myself because I didn't see the warning signs. I kept thinking, *"What are the odds of my first love just happening to be an abusive man and him turning out to be the biggest jackass I had ever met?"*

I began to get sick to my stomach to know that the man I fell in love with had turn out to be such a failure in our marriage. I was so naïve back then I thought to myself no one should own a person's life, but I wasn't doing anything about it. I knew that the bible said when two people are joined together, they become as one flesh. But that didn't mean that your spouse should beat or control you like a puppet. I had never liked to be controlled, but because I was so scared of my husband at the time, I didn't know what else to do at that point. I knew I had to come up with a plan to leave him before he killed me. I wasn't sure how I was going to leave without getting caught. I knew whatever I did I had to be very careful because my husband was very smart. He was always one step ahead of me with his bag of tricks.

I was determined to get help. It took me awhile before I was able to tell my parents that Adam was beating me, and that he had threatened to kill me. I decided that the next time that we visited my parents, I was going to somehow get my mom to go into the bedroom so I could talk to Mom alone. I was

Wounds
For Love Comes Tragic and Painful

so nervous, I felt so ashamed, scared, and embarrassed to tell Mom. I had never said anything to anyone about it. While my dad and my husband were talking, my mom and I went into their bedroom to talk, and I told my mom that my husband had beat me. When we left my parents house, I knew that my husband would want to know what my mom and I were talking about. I could tell that my mom wasn't happy about what my husband did to me, and I knew Mom would tell my dad. Dad wasn't the kind of man to play around with when it came down to his family. I remember telling my husband that my mom wanted to show me her new dress that she had bought, because she wanted to know what kind shoes to get to wear with it. I was never good at lying, but I had to this time.

I felt that Mom and I weren't very close, but that didn't stop me from telling her what my husband had done to me. I remember when we got home, my husband beat me again because I had went into my parent's bedroom to talk to Mom. After the beating, he told me that the next time we went over to my parent's house, he wanted me to sit in the same room as him. So after that, I couldn't talk to my mother anymore because he was always there seated next to me at their house.

-Let He who is Without Sin -

My parents knew that he was beating me, but they didn't know that he was raping me. I had kept that a secret from everyone. I remember the time we went to visit his brother and his wife and he told me that he didn't want me talking too much. When we were on our way home from visiting his brother's house, there was another car that pulled up on the side of us at the light. My eyes had glanced over to the car next to us. I remember my husband started accusing me of knowing the man in the car next to us. I couldn't even look outside my window without him getting jealous. I hadn't paid any attention to the man in the car next to us, but my husband didn't believe me. When we got home, he starting beating me saying he wanted me to tell him who the man was in the car next to us. I kept telling Adam that I had never saw the man before. I was so sure that he was going to kill me that day over some stupid shit behind his jealousy. I always had been confident in myself but now, all of my esteem was missing. I felt that I was damned if do and damned if I don't. I just could not seem to please him. I was getting sick and tired of him always getting mad all the time and I was the one being punished; this was all of his bullshit, I thought, especially every time he beat me up and then said he was sorry. I wished I had a dollar for every time my husband said that he was sorry to me. At least then, I would have gotten paid for the ass whippings.

WOUNDS
FOR LOVE COMES TRAGIC AND PAINFUL

I knew my husband was lying because that was his favorite word, that he was "sorry" afterward. I couldn't believe how many nights I was supposed to be sleeping but instead I was always stressed in pain and suffering, restless over some foolish shit.

The abuse went on for months, and finally I got a job working in Opelousas, Louisiana. We lived about ten or fifteen minutes away from Opelousas. There was a new drug store that was hiring people to help stock merchandise on the shelves to get ready for their grand opening of the business. I was glad that I found a job, so I didn't have to be home alone all the time, waiting on my husband hand and foot. Besides, this was to be my first real job! I remember my first day on the job; my husband let me drive the car to work. I noticed when it was time to get off work that one of the tires was on flat. My husband was still at work, so I called him to tell him that I had a flat tire, and I needed him to come and get it fixed. When he got there, he immediately accused me of flirting with one of the guys that I worked with. I told him that I wasn't flirting with anyone, but he didn't believe me. My husband was driving his motorcycle at the time and he wanted to know how the air got out of the tire. He believed that one of the guys that I was flirting with might have let the air out of the tire. I didn't know how the tire got flat, but I also knew that I hadn't flirted with any of the guys at work. When we got home from work, we had to get ready for church that evening. After church on our way home, we stopped off at my parent's house. It was late so we didn't stay very long. I told my parents that I had started a new job working for a drug store and on my first day the car had a flat. When we left from visiting my parents, Adam started asking me again who I was flirting with at work. I told him again that I wasn't flirting with anyone at work and that no one had let the air out. When we got home that evening, Adam kept pressuring me to tell him who the guy was I was flirting with. I was getting ready for bed; it was late, and we had to go to work the next morning. After I had gotten into bed, he then grabbed one of my legs and started pulling and twisting my ankle with his hand until he sprung my ankle. My ankle hurt so bad, I thought that he had broken it; I was in so much pain.

The next morning when we got up to go to work, we noticed that the same tire that he fixed the night before was on a flat again. Now who was looking stupid that morning? He was! I had gotten my ankle sprung for nothing. He couldn't say a thing because he found out the tire had a slow leak. I remember being so mad that I wanted to beat the living day lights out of my husband so he could experience the pain that he put me though. I had to go to work with a sprung ankle, staying on my feet all

WOUNDS
FOR LOVE COMES TRAGIC AND PAINFUL

day long working because of his foolishness. Now I recalled on that day, my parents were in town taking care of some business. On their way home, my parent's stopped by to see how I was doing. I told my parents that Adam had twisted my ankle until he sprung it. My dad noticed that my ankle was swollen so he went back in to town, and bought a wrap for my ankle to ease some of the pain. I heard my mom saying to my dad that I knew he was going to do something to her. At that moment, I knew in her heart that she loved me and was concerned. My parents were noticeably upset about him hurting me, especially my dad. I could see the look on his face. If looks could kill, my husband would have been dead then, but Dad didn't say anything. I knew my parents loved me, even though they might not have said it. I could see it in their eyes.

    There was one Friday night I wanted the twins to spend the night with me. At the time, they were about four years. I was so happy that my parents had let the twins spend the night with us that night. I had not only loved them, but I had spoiled them as well; they were like my own children. When we got home that night, I started cooking dinner while my husband and the twins were watching television. When dinner was ready, I fixed the twins food first. Then I fixed my husband's food shortly afterward. When the twins were finished eating, they had stayed up for a little while as I was cleaning up in the kitchen. Then I got them ready for bed afterwards. I went into the bedroom to get ready for bed myself as my husband was still watching television in the living room. I noticed that my husband walked in the bedroom, and as I was turning to get in the bed, he punched me so hard and fast, I didn't see it coming. He tried to corner me in by the dresser in our room. As I was trying to get away, he kept on punching me again and again.

I was trying not to make too much noise so the twins wouldn't wake up. I didn't want the twins to see my husband beating me up. He had a funky attitude because I had fixed the twins food before I fixed his food, and for that, he beat me. He also had his hand over my mouth so I couldn't scream. He told me that if I screamed, he would kill me. I was trying not to make any noise because I knew that the twins were just in the other room, and I was scared because I had the twins. I didn't want the twins to get hurt over some stupid and dumb shit that my husband was doing to me. After he beat me, he then threw me on the bed and raped me. When he finished raping me, he went back into the living room and watched TV like nothing happened.

Wounds
For Love Comes Tragic and Painful

He didn't need to rape me when I was willing to give it to him. Maybe he thought that made him more of a man when he had to take it with his knife to my throat. I was tired of crying and being unhappy with this sorry excuse for a man, and I was sick of listening to his sorry excuses afterwards.

I never knew where he kept his knife hidden. At times I saw him put under his pillow, and he guarded it with his life. In the morning, when he got up for work, I would search for it when he was in the bathroom, but I could never find it. I knew he had taken it to work with him.

I knew love was a lot of things but not this; who in their right mind would sign up for this kind of love for the rest of their life? That was a death sentence waiting to happen. I felt my husband didn't have the right to hold my life in his hand. My husband was on the usher board at the church and none of the members knew this other side of him.

I can remember there were times when my husband came home from work that he could be such a loving and caring person to me. There were moments when we would actually talk, laugh, and we would have so much fun together. It seemed as if things were normal between us, but the truth was, I wasn't happy. I had learned to pretend to be happy, and even that wasn't enough because I knew it wouldn't last long. He would soon be back to his old self again. Things were far from normal. I still had to be careful what I said or did around him. Any sign or abnormal reaction would set him off, and I didn't want that to happen.

I remember one time when we were both in the living room watching television one night. It was around the month of October. He had said that he was not going to abuse me again. It was after church that day. When we came home from church that evening, we were seated there watching television in the living room. I was curled up in a chair with a pillow around my stomach watching TV with my feet up in the chair. He had been on the couch. He got up and walked passed me, and stabbed me on my right thumb with the same hunting knife. He pretended to be going to our bedroom as he passed very quickly by me and stabbed me. I was bleeding everywhere. I was glad I had that pillow in front of my stomach or otherwise he would have stabbed me in the stomach with the knife.

He was saying he was sorry, but he didn't want to take me to the hospital. I had to beg him to take me. Finally my husband agreed to take me after he

Wounds
For Love Comes Tragic and Painful

begged me not to leave him or tell anyone what had happened. He waited hours until late that night before he would take me. Now, he was scared and nervous because he knew they would ask me how did this happen. I was in pain, and this fool even made me drive myself to the hospital. Then he started again with being sorry, up until the time we arrived at the hospital. Then he started acting like he was the one who had been stabbed. We lived in Grand Prairie, Louisiana and the closest hospital was in Opelousas, Louisiana and he made me drive while he sat on the passenger side. When we arrived at the emergency room, the nurse was assisting with the stab wound. She asked me what happened, and I had to lie because my husband was standing right next to me. I told the nurse that I cut myself with a knife when I was washing dishes.

While the nurse was cleaning my wound out, she told me that I was going to need four or five stitches on my right thumb. My stupid idiot husband fainted – passed out right on the floor. I remember being so angry with him saying to myself, *"Look at this fool; I am the one with the stab wound and in pain for his bullshit! But yet, he is the one fainting at the sight of blood!"* The nurse had to stop what she was doing to help my husband up and tend to his needs while I was in pain. I was furious because he had made me wait that late before taking me to the hospital and not to mention I had to drive myself while he sat on the passenger side. When the nurse was done taking care of my husband in the other room, then I was able to finished getting stitches. Then, on the way home, I also had to drive myself home that night while my husband was sitting on the passenger side again. I felt weak, and helpless to the point that I started to feel hate in my heart for my husband. I couldn't believe how he acted at the hospital when all this was his fault that we had to go to the hospital in the first place. On our way home, he started crying like a baby for me not to leave him. We are almost home and it was pretty dark on those country roads; we didn't have much street lights back then. Just when I thought that things couldn't get any worse, then my husband decided to jump out of the moving car because I was going to leave him. I remember thinking this idiot husband of mine has jumped out of a moving vehicle because I'm talking about leaving him. I wished just for that moment that I could have beaten the living daylights out of him for jumping out of the car putting on a pitiful act for me not to leave him.

Adam knew that night I was fed up, sick and tired of his bullshit. I didn't know how much more I could take from him. When I stopped the car to find out what was his problem, he then refused to get back in the car until I promised him that I wasn't going to

WOUNDS
FOR LOVE COMES TRAGIC AND PAINFUL

leave him. He then told me to drive the car while he held on to the back of the car. I wished that I could have left him there, but I knew that would only make things worse for me. I agreed to stay if he promised to change his ways – meaning the abuse and threats that he had been making on my life. I told him if it continued I would be gone for good. He promised to stop. I wasn't sure if he would keep his promise, but I knew I was fed up all of the crazy nonsense he was doing to me. I told Adam that I just couldn't do this anymore. I was to the point where I felt I was losing my mind, and that he had pushed me to the limit. I knew something had to give and I wasn't accepting his sorrowful pity parties anymore. I told him some changes had to be made and he agreed. I remember being so exhausted and tired that night when we got home, I went straight to bed and fell asleep. The next morning my husband was so happy that I didn't leave him so now he was trying to make up to me for all the things he had done. I remember thinking that next day after my husband left for work that I had seen a store down the road when we were on our way home the night before. I thought just in case my husband decided to do something stupid again, I would have a backup plan. I wasn't sure if there was a pay phone or not, but I was determined to find a way just in case he didn't keep his word. I knew that the store was far to walk, but I was going to take that chance if I had to while my husband was at work. I had no money and I wasn't sure if they had a pay phone but I was determined to give it a try even if I had to make the call collect to my parent's house.

When I got to the store, there was a pay phone and I was able to make that collect call to my parent's house. My mom answered the phone and I told mom that I needed my dad to come and get me and he did. When my husband got home from work and realized I was gone, he rushed over to my parents house begging me to come back home. But, I wouldn't go with him. I remember he came to my parent's house everyday to get me to come home. One day when I didn't agree to come home, he tried to take my mom's medicine that was on the bar. He pretended to try to act like he was going to kill himself by taking my mom's medicine all because I would not come back home with him that day.

My parents and I couldn't believe how stupid and crazy he was acting on that day. They were very angry with him. I didn't know what to do; I was even more scared now to go back. My parents talked to me about what I wanted to do. The very next day he came over again. I remember my dad having a very long talk with my husband about him beating me. I began to think I wanted my marriage to work. I had given it some serious thought for about a week when

WOUNDS
FOR LOVE COMES TRAGIC AND PAINFUL

by then, I had decided to go back and make it work. It was something about seeing him and my dad talking together that night. I felt that my husband was threatened or intimated by my dad in some way, so now that my dad had this long talk with my husband, I felt that he might do better, so I would give our marriage a chance. I also recall my dad telling my husband if he laid his hand on me again that he would have to deal with him. I knew my dad was very serious, and he wasn't the type of man to play around. I told my husband that I would only go back if he agreed to change or else I wasn't going back, so he agreed to change. Although I wasn't sure if he meant it, at the time I was going to give him a chance to prove himself to me.

After Dad's long talk with my husband, I could tell that he acted all nervous when he was around my dad. I also could tell that he had respect for my dad. I think that is the reason he didn't want my parents to know he was abusing me. He didn't know that they already knew. I felt safe at my parent's house. I didn't have to be afraid or scared at night over there. When I came back to our home though, I was just devastated over all of the abuse. My mind was messed up and my heart was broken. I couldn't get a grip on things. Many nights I cried myself to sleep feeling helpless and wondering how my life got so out of control in the short time we were married. I saw myself as a failure; I was disappointed in myself for not being very strong. I felt ashamed and angry at myself. I knew I was very tired of the same old song and dance routine with my husband. I'd hope the talk my dad had with my husband would work and then maybe things could be different between us. I wanted to make our marriage work, but I was still afraid of him. Then finally, I was also worried about what folks would say, since we were still newlyweds. No one but my parents knew what was going on, and I was too ashamed to tell anyone else. I had become very numb inside.

I had never experienced anything like that in my life because I hadn't seen anyone in my family go through this kind of abuse. I feel if I hadn't been so naïve or sheltered too much, maybe this wouldn't have happened to me. I never saw my dad put his hand on my mom, or for that matter, I'd never seen them have a fight. There were times when they argued, and even then, they didn't do it in front of me and my siblings. Growing up I always thought that my parents had a good marriage; I remember thinking some day when I got married, I wanted my marriage to be strong like theirs, and here I am married for a couple of months and things were already out of control. That was the reason I was determined to make my marriage work. I knew marriage was a full time job just like anything in life worth saving.

WOUNDS
FOR LOVE COMES TRAGIC AND PAINFUL

    I could also tell that my mom was worried about me going back to him, but I knew that was a mother's job to worry about her children, no matter how old the children were. I knew mothers always had a way of knowing when their child was hurting or in pain, even though I didn't say anything, she knew. My dad was also not happy with the way my husband treated me; I could tell by the look on his face. My dad was angry with my husband even when he tried not to show it. I knew my dad wasn't a violent man, but when it came down to protecting his family and love ones, look out! I had never seen my dad fight with anyone. A person would have to make him pretty damn mad for him to do something to them.

    I had lost all respect for my husband as a man. I thought he would have to earn my respect back because I still didn't trust him anymore. Because I was raised in the church, I was not only praying for my marriage to work but I was also stepping out on faith to pull me through this situation. That was my first time as an adult stepping out in faith to trust God for something. I believed in God and marriage, and I believed in my heart that this marriage should and could work. I remember my husband was trying to be nice to me after I had gone back home with him. I'd hoped that things would change for good.

-LET HE WHO IS WITHOUT SIN -

Well a couple months went by and things were getting better. I was still having a hard time with his jealous complaints all the time, I was also dealing with some mental issues that I was going through in my own head because he had torn me down so. It was hard for me to get my spirits back up. At the time he wasn't physically abusing me, but he was still abusing me mentally.

The holidays were coming up and things were still good between us. We still had a ways to go but at least he wasn't beating me. I noticed even our sex life had gotten better; he was making love to me and not raping me. I was so happy about that. I also noticed during that time that I was getting sick a lot. I didn't know what was going on until I realize that I might be pregnant, and I knew it was time for me to see a doctor. I went to the doctor, and it was confirmed that I was pregnant. I remember being happy in one way but concerned at the same time. I knew that I always wanted children of my own someday, but not at the expense of bringing a child into an abusive relationship. When I told my parents that I was pregnant, they were happy for me, but at the same time concerned that there grandchild would be exposed to some kind of violence and abuse.

WOUNDS
FOR LOVE COMES TRAGIC AND PAINFUL

We got through Christmas and the New Year was right around the corner when I noticed that my husband's attitude was beginning to change again, I could see by the way he was talking that his jealous rage and threatening words are starting to come back – this time in full force. I was sitting there thinking to myself, "Well, he's back to his old self again; I was wondering how long the fun would last."

Two months into the pregnancy and I was hoping that Adam wouldn't try to abuse me, especially since I was pregnant. I knew that I wasn't going to let him beat me while I was pregnant. I decided that wasn't going to happen. I had become very worried at that point what he might do, and I was still insecure about myself, not to mention I was trying to get my self esteem back. I was tired of being on a rollercoaster ride with my husband. Then came three months into my pregnancy and my husband had come home from work with an attitude again. He was upset about something and he decided he wanted to take it out on me. I remember telling him that I wasn't going to let him beat me, especially now that I was pregnant.

That is the same day I wasn't feeling well so I hadn't cooked. That made him more furious with me because I didn't cook on that day. He then raised his voice at me and tried to torment me just by dogging me out saying that he was going to kill me and kill the baby. I finally found the strength to put my foot down and tell my husband, *"No more! It would have to be over my dead body."* I remember him hitting me and me asking him to stop. He asked me who was going to stop him. I then said to him that I'd rather he kill me because I was tired of being tormented by him every day. Even though I was a very strong person before, in that short time I was married to my husband, he had stripped me of all my dignity, pride, integrity, self-respect, self-esteem, and security. I refused to continue to be a victim. I was going to put a stop to it even if it meant me and my unborn child's life. I figured what else did I have to lose? I had never hated anyone that much before in my life! At that point, I couldn't stand the sight of him anymore. I told my husband that he might as well go ahead and kill me; at least I wouldn't have to deal with him abusing me anymore! I felt at least I would be free and at peace from him. He already had put a distance between me and my family, and I felt I had nothing else to lose.

I was determined to leave him for good this time because of my unborn child. I knew I had to be very careful getting the message to my mom for my dad to come and get me when he came home from offshore. I managed to get the message to Mom. It was set. I knew what day Dad was coming to pick me

WOUNDS
FOR LOVE COMES TRAGIC AND PAINFUL

up. So I waited until my husband left for work that morning before I began packing my bag. I had no idea what time my dad was coming to pick me up, but I was ready and waiting for my dad when he showed up. It was Thursday afternoon, March 19, 1981. My dad had gone home first, and then went to visit his parents. My dad always visited his parents when he came home from working offshore. He and his brothers always would help my grandfather out with chopping wood for the fireplaces and help out around the house.

It was a little after lunchtime when my dad arrived. Within minutes after my dad arrived and entered into the house, my husband rushed into the house very quickly from work wanting to know what was going on. He had seen when my dad drove by. At the time my husband was working close to the road that led to our house and he could see the cars and trucks go by from the road. I told him that I was leaving; I had my bag packed and ready to go. I could see the look on my husband's face and knew that something was going to happen as he was very upset now. He wanted to talk, but when I wanted to talk before, all he wanted to do was beat the hell out me for no reason. Now he wanted to talk, – but it was too late. All I could think of was that he could go to hell as far as I was concerned. I was sick and tired of him saying that he was sorry. I hated him for what he had put me through. That was the last straw. I didn't know how to get a handle on my emotional feelings that were out of control. I had so much going on in my head. My husband had made my life a living hell in the nine months that we were married, and I felt he had given me a lifetime of pain and misery. My husband was trying to get me to stay, but I knew that he wasn't going to change, and my dad could see that I was getting nowhere with my husband.

Dad was a very loving and caring man; he also was a very patient man. Even when my husband was trying to talk me into staying, Dad had sat there on the couch waiting on me not saying a word. As I grabbed my bag to leave, my husband wouldn't let me leave with my bag. My dad saw that I was getting nowhere with my husband, so he stood and told me to leave the bag. Dad could see that my husband was getting very upset at the time. I recall that my dad told me to leave my bag, and that we would come back later with the police to get my things, so I did. Dad was a very peaceful man; he didn't like to cause any trouble, only when it came down to someone hurting his children or loved ones – watch out! My dad had parked his truck right next to the steps of our house, so it was easy to just get in the truck. As I and my dad headed toward the door to the truck, my husband was still standing in the house. Dad went to open the door on the driver's side of the truck, and I

WOUNDS
FOR LOVE COMES TRAGIC AND PAINFUL

was already opening the door on the passenger side. All of a sudden, my husband ran out of the house very quickly on my dad's side of the truck toward the road. I was wondering what my husband was doing running toward the road. In that split second, my dad opened his truck door; he told me that my husband had stabbed him. I couldn't believe that I was hearing my dad say that he was stabbed! I thought, *"Now I know my husband is crazy!"* I rushed over to the driver's side while Dad stumbled over to the passenger's side. As I proceeded to get in the truck to drive off, I saw the knife on the floor of the truck! My dad had pulled the knife out of his side and laid it down on the floor of the truck. I noticed that it was the same knife that my husband had stabbed me with months earlier.

Now, I really knew that my husband had lost his mind! I was in shock! I didn't know how to process what had just happened, but I knew I had to get my dad to the hospital very quickly. My leaving triggered his violent rage to the point of no return. I didn't know what to do at that point. I was tired of playing games with my husband. I knew I had to pull myself together and drive my dad to the hospital. As I was backing out onto the road, my husband was still standing at the end of the drive way when he jumped into the tail of my dad's moving truck.

- Let He who is Without Sin -

When he jumped into the tail of my dad's truck while I was backing out, he picked up the axe that was in the tail of my dad's truck. He told me to stop the truck or he would kill me with my dad's axe. I was thinking he would just have to kill me because I wasn't stopping. When he saw that I wasn't going to stop, then he told me that he wanted to help. I thought he had done enough already so I would not stop. He then jumped out of the truck. In that moment, I knew I didn't need his help! He had already done enough damage to me and my family.

As I was driving Dad to the hospital, I could see that he was in so much pain. His head was leaning on my right side. I was driving so fast. I felt like I had lost my mind. I felt numb all over. It was like I was having an out of body experience and I was in a trance. I kept hearing my dad say he wanted to go home and I kept telling him that I had to take him to the hospital first. I also noticed that it seemed like it was taking me a very long time to get to the hospital. I recall that I didn't even have my purse, but I kept on driving. My mind was focused on getting my dad to the hospital even though he wanted me to take him home. I had to convince him that I was going to take him to the hospital first, and then we could go home. I could see he was struggling to survive, and he was in extreme pain by the way his head kept leaning on my side, making a snoring sound. He also couldn't sit

WOUNDS
FOR LOVE COMES TRAGIC AND PAINFUL

straight. I finally got dad to agree to let me take him to the hospital, and I remember driving him all the way to Ville Platte General Hospital. I couldn't even think straight to drive him to the Opelousas hospital which would have been quicker. When I got there, I was still not thinking straight. I dropped him off at the emergency room. Then I got back into the truck and rushed over to my mom's job to tell her that my dad was stabbed, and that I had dropped him off to the hospital. I rushed back to the hospital not thinking that I could have called my mom's job instead.

This was a small town and news travels fast whether it is good or bad. I remember when my mom got there, she was trying to ask my dad if he had left the door unlocked for the twins. They were only five years old at the time. Mom was trying to find out if dad had left the door unlocked for the twins to get in the house since they had just started school, and there would be no one to let them in the house. Mom wasn't getting a good response from Dad because he was in and out of it. Within hours some of our family members were arriving at the hospital waiting to find out about my dad's condition and how serious was his wound. While his nurse was doing everything she could, my mom was talking to my dad until his doctor arrived. It seemed to be taking forever for the doctor to get there.

CAST THE FIRST STONE

That day was the worst day of my life. I was just in shock. My mind starting having all those mixed emotions running around in my head. I just couldn't believe that my husband would do something like that to me and my family. I had never been so terrified, humiliated, and embarrassed in my life. I just couldn't think straight for what my husband had done to my father. I couldn't do anything but sit there with my family. I remember so many things were running through my mind. I felt helpless! I remember sitting in the waiting room with my uncle feeling sorry because it was my fault that my dad was in the hospital. I also recall telling my uncle that my dad wasn't going to make it, and my uncle said that he would be fine.

I could tell that my uncle didn't understand what I was meant at the time. I knew he was trying to comfort me, but I knew better. I knew in heart that my dad wasn't going to make it. I kept having a funny feeling in my head and I couldn't shake it off. The doctor finally arrived to do surgery on my dad. Minutes after the doctor took him into the operating room, I and my family was seated in the waiting room when the police showed up to question me

Wounds
For Love Comes Tragic and Painful

about what happened to my dad. Right when the policeman was finished talking to us, the doctor came out and told my mom that my dad didn't make it. He died right when they opened him up for surgery on the operating room table. It was only five minutes later that the doctor came out of surgery, but it seemed like it happened in a split-second. I was thinking they got through so fast. But then, I realized that my dad was gone.

When the doctor told my mom that dad didn't make it, I heard my mom screaming and crying in a sound that I had never heard her sound like that before. Then all of my family as well started crying out who was sitting there with us at the time. All of the other family members were crying when they heard the news of my dad's death. I couldn't believe that he was gone just that quickly. I remember being stricken with grief and I couldn't even imagine how my mom was feeling. At that point, family members were trying to comfort my mom. I felt a ton of bricks had fallen on my heart and crushed me. I was in a state of shock at that moment. I was in so much pain all I could do was cry and wish it was me and not my dad. I felt this was my entire fault that my dad was dead. Within that moment, I felt like a part of me had died as well. That was my first stone.

-Cast the First Stone-

I had never experienced anything like that in my life. Never in a million years did I imagine having a loved one in my family to die at the hand of my husband. I felt so ashamed and embarrassed that I couldn't face my mom or her family. My dad died at 5:30 p.m. on March 19, 1981; that was on a Thursday evening.

The doctor told me and my mom that because my dad was stabbed in his liver, it had caused him to suffocate. His food hadn't had time to digest. The doctor also told us that if my dad would have lived, he would only be a vegetable and I knew my family didn't want that for my dad. That would be painful for my family to see him like that. We left the hospital with so much pain inside; no one could even imagine what was going through our hearts and minds at that time.

When Mom and I arrived at home, the first thing we noticed was the grandfather clocks and all the other clocks in the house had stopped at the same time that my dad died. That was one of the strangest things that we had ever seen. Then family members started pouring in. The news of my dad's death had traveled fast. People from all over were showing up to give their support to the family. We had family members coming to extend their deepest sympathy

Wounds
For Love Comes Tragic and Painful

and their prayers in our time of sorrow at the loss of my dad. My family was not only shocked, but devastated by the news. Considering my dad and his family were very close to one another, and he had just seen his parents earlier that day, who knew that day was going to be the last time that they would see or talk to their son alive just hours before his death? I had no idea that this would be the last time that I would ever see or talk to my dad again. I had no idea how I was going to make it without my dad. I could not even begin to understand how my mom was would ever get through this.

When my mom entered into their bedroom coming in from the hospital, she saw that the bed wasn't fixed that day. She began to cry all over again. My dad had never made it back home on that day to make the bed; my mom had asked him to take the sheets off the bed to be washed. My mom said that was first time in the nineteen years her and my dad was married that the bed hadn't been fixed the whole day. When my dad would come home from offshore he usually helped out around the house with the cooking and cleaning. He also would go over to his parents' house to visit and help my grandfather chop wood for the fireplaces. He always had his axes in the tail of the truck. My dad was always helping someone or somebody; that was the kind of man he was, and that was what I loved about my dad. He was the kind of man that liked helping others. He didn't care who that person was; that was his gift. As I was noticing my mom taking this very hard, I could see that she was in so much pain, and there was nothing I could do to ease her pain. I didn't know how my mom was going to cope with my dad gone and all since he would take care of everything; I felt so ashamed. I felt that it was all my fault. I was willing to take the blame for my dad's death. I was devastated, confused, lost, angry, and very disappointed in myself because as much as I loved my dad, I didn't know what I was going to do now that he was gone. I found myself wishing that it was me that had died and not my dad because he had a wife, and a family that was left behind with no one to take care of them. I felt that I not only failed myself, but also my family as well because of my idiot husband. I had lost everything just that quick! I never knew what real pain was until I lost my dad. All I wanted to do was die; I was just a few months pregnant now and my whole world was turned upside down just in that short time. I didn't know how to cope or deal with all the pain my husband had caused me and my family. I could not imagine me ever being a victim of domestic violence or abuse before. That was so devastating to me to the point where I became so angry and bitter within myself. I really felt responsible for my dad's death. That is the reason I was ashamed; if it wasn't for me, he would still be alive.

WOUNDS
FOR LOVE COMES TRAGIC AND PAINFUL

Now my mom is making funeral arrangements for my dad who was only thirty seven years old at the time of his death. The day of the funeral I had seen so many people that my dad had touched. There were so many folks there, even white folks. That is how much he was loved and is missed. The funeral was on a Monday morning; it was a sad funeral. That same day the weather was bad; it rained all day. I was able to go to the funeral but my family wouldn't let me go to the cemetery because I was pregnant. Back then the older generation believed if a person had any kind of surgery, open cut wound, or pregnancy, you weren't allowed to go to the cemetery until those things were healed. After the funeral, family member were pouring in to help us go through life's greatest sorrow and to offer their support. When all of the family members had gone home, we were left to face the reality that he was never coming back. It was hard for me and my family to pick up the pieces when we didn't know how. Sometime I felt like I didn't know how to go on with my life with my dad was gone and never coming back. Over the weeks, there were times when I would look at my mom, and I could see how much pain I had caused my mother with my dad gone and all. Considering that my mom was still in so much pain, I felt like my mom would never get over this. Although I knew my mom was a pretty strong woman, sometimes I thought I would die when I could hear my mother crying from her room. There was nothing I could do to ease her pain; I was totally useless. There were times when I was so ashamed and I didn't know how or what to say to my mom. Of course, I blamed myself for what happened. Even though I knew that my mom didn't blame me, I could see all the pain my mom was in and I only wished that I could ease her pain. I felt some sense of responsibility because now my mother didn't have a husband and my brother and sisters didn't have a father.

    I felt I'd lost everything. I didn't just lose Dad; I lost my family too. I'd lost my dignity, pride, self-respect, integrity, hope, joy, peace, and my esteem; they were all gone. I thought here I am pregnant living with my mom and my brother and sisters with all the pain wrapped up inside of me. Not knowing how to cope with all that pain, I had lost myself! All I could do was cry all the time. I didn't want anyone to see me breakdown, so I would hold everything inside of me until I got in the room. I also didn't want to see or talk to anyone. I had become very reserved dealing with things in my own way. I didn't talk at all about what I was going through. I was so numb, and I felt that no one understood anyway.

Live to Tell

Thirty years have passed since my dad's murder, thirty-three years since the day I mistakenly disconnected the phone call from my mother. His death was the first of my "stones." I call them stones because they are the "hard places" of my life. These were times that were so terrible that I learned how to suppress them for years rather than deal with them. I just kept crying and cutting myself with stones for thirty years after dad's death. I have still not quite been able to reconcile why I sometimes feel mentally disconnected from my family. I have never been able to freely express to my mom or anyone else in my family for that matter how I felt – the pain, the hurt, and the guilt I felt because of what happened. When I was sixteen and I accidentally hollered, "Bitch!" over the phone to my mother on the other end – that was an accident – an innocent mistake that I could explain, and live to laugh about afterwards.

My father's death however, was not something I could live down. Yes, I was innocent – completely and totally ignorant of the monster that I married. But that didn't change the fact that even after my divorce from that crazy man, my dad was still gone. Me, my younger sisters and brother, as well as my mother, and entire family – all of whom I dearly loved – were robbed of the father we so loved, cherished, and admired.

Even though that monster took him from us, to me, it felt like I inflicted the fatal wound. How could I have chosen this kind of person to marry? Was I so lovesick or starved for validation that I did not see any signs?

Ignorance and naivety led me to tragedy and pain. I had lost my virginity to my husband on our wedding night; I loved him! But in less than 24 hours later, I had gone from being an eighteen-year old blissful beautiful bride to a savagely raped and beaten scorned woman. The older generation had nothing but prayer and patience; they were able to endure until their answer came through prayer. I didn't know what to do.

I was more concerned about my mother, my brother, Jay (being an only son), and my little sisters at the time. I felt so devastated and humiliated that my family had to go through all of the pain and hurt. I wished that I could turn back the clock. I just kept thinking, "What about my mom? What about my family? Look at all the pain this has caused them!"

WOUNDS
FOR LOVE COMES TRAGIC AND PAINFUL

After Dad died, someone in the family took me and my mother to the doctor, and the doctor told my family that I had suffered a nervous breakdown. The doctor also told them that I needed some help. But I didn't get any help. I just dealt with everything the best way I could, even though I was in so much pain. I remember folk used to say, *"God doesn't put any more on you than you can bear."* I didn't know what to believe then, but today I know that God didn't put that burden on me at all. That horror was not from God. He doesn't operate like that. At the time, my heart was so full that I felt God had forgotten about me, and I was angry with God for leaving me and taking my dad away from my family. Because my heart was so heavy and full, I had no way of releasing all of the pressure that was weighing me down. I was filled with so much guilt and shame that the weight on my shoulders became too hard to carry. I didn't know what I was going to do. Now that I was pregnant with no father and no husband, I felt like I was cursed. It seemed that one minute I had everything and the next minute, I lost everything, except for my unborn child.

Three weeks went by and I was still grieving. Then we faced another death in the family – that was when my dad's sister, Aunt Lynn, Aunt Glenda's twin – the one with breast cancer died. She was my dad's godchild. I became even more devastated. Again, I started questioning why God was putting so much on me. I felt like my heart had been torn into a million pieces. I just didn't have any more room in my heart to store anymore pain or hurt. I felt my heart was going to burst wide opened. I had lost the will to live. I saw my mom was trying to be strong to take care of her children, and I knew it was not easy. When family members came over to see how we were holding up, I would stay in the room until they were gone.

Months went by, but the pain and the hurt was still there every time I looked into my mother's eyes, I could see all the pain and hurt that I'd caused her. I was about seven months pregnant now and I was still having a hard time dealing with my dad and aunt's death. This time was a huge blow to the whole family. I recalled my mom saying to me during that time that she wasn't going to help take care of my child. My mother had asked me what I was going to do to raise my child when I didn't even have a job. My mom was right. How was I going to raise my child? I couldn't blame my mother for talking to me and feeling the way she did. She had every right to feel that way. I understood that she was still going through a grieving process over her husband's death. I didn't know what I would have done had I been in my mom's shoes. I was still going through the grieving process as well, and I was not thinking about what I was going to do to take care of my child. I was living with my mom

WOUNDS
FOR LOVE COMES TRAGIC AND PAINFUL

and my siblings at the time, and I knew that everything was very hard for my mom, knowing that I was pregnant with no husband and a baby on the way with my dad gone.

A few weeks later, I started having some pain during the day. I knew that it was not time for me to have the baby. That same day, my Aunt Renada had come to spend the night with us. My Aunt Renada was my mom's baby sister. She and I were sharing the same bed in the bedroom that night. During the middle of the night, I started having more pain. I remember getting up trying to get to my mom's bedroom, but by that time, I was in so much pain that I had to use the bathroom. When I walked into my mom's bathroom at the time, I recall trying to make it back to my mom's bedroom when I realized that my water bag had broken. I crawled over to my mom's bed to tell her that I needed to go to the hospital. I knew my mom wouldn't be too happy about getting out of bed late at night, But my mom did get up and take me to the hospital. It was the same hospital where my dad died. We didn't really have a choice in that small town. I knew that it would be very painful for my mother to handle going back to the same hospital where my dad had died just five months earlier. I knew it was hard for me, so I knew it was hard for her to handle as well, but this was the closest hospital.

When my mother took me to the hospital, she didn't stay with me. I knew my mom had to work the next morning so she left when they took me to the delivery room. I was all alone. Within minutes, I had a baby girl. I recall seeing my baby's head at the time of her delivery, and she had lots of hair on her head. That was the only thing I could notice because my looking was interrupted by the doctor talking. The doctor said that my baby was already dead and the umbilical cord was wrapped around her neck. I was struck with hurt and pain all over again. The doctor used the term stillborn. I remember crying out loud so much that the doctor had to give me a shot to calm me down. Now I had lost my daughter, my dad, and my aunt all within three months. I felt lost. Now, I had nothing else left. All of my hope and faith was completely gone. The next morning when I woke up, I felt so alone and empty inside that all I wanted to do was die. All of this had left a big hole in my heart. On that morning, I remember asking the doctor if there was any way that I could see my baby girl, and I was told that my family had already left to do the burial.

I was devastated! I had no one left it seemed. I felt numb inside and on top of that, no one came to visit me and offer their support. I remember walking up and down the hospital hall with my head down filled with so much guilt and shame. I was told that my brother had buried my daughter right next to my

Wounds
For Love Comes Tragic and Painful

dad. I was hurt because I hadn't even gotten to give my daughter a name. When I asked my brother what was my daughter's name, he couldn't even remember! Then, I got that much more upset! I felt like they had just buried my daughter next to my dad's grave with no headstone – not even a cross was put on her. It was like she didn't matter at all – but she did matter to me.

Although I was in pain over the loss of my daughter, later on, I started to feel that maybe it was best that my daughter was dead because I didn't want anyone to resent my daughter for something that my husband had done. I was very upset and angry all at the same time. My heart was aching so badly after I lost my baby; I didn't know what I was going to do now. While I was still in the hospital, a few days or so had passed. I was walking in the hospital hallway with my head hung down when two guys coming to visit their sister came by my room. Her room was next to mine, and they spoke to me as I was walking with my head down. I recall a little later that one of the guys knocked on my door and asked if he could sit with me. I remember the guy's name was Ken. He asked me if he could sit with me for a while. I said yes that it was ok. He had asked me what I was in the hospital for, so I told him that I had just lost my baby. He told me that he was sorry for my loss. I asked Ken who was he and his brother coming to visit. He said his sister. He then asked if he could visit me the next day if I was still in the hospital. I hesitated, and then I said yes. At the time, I was not sure if I wanted him to be my friend because I was going though so much and I was in so much pain at the time. I was hurting inside not ready to open up to any new friends, although at the time, I didn't have any friends to talk to. I wasn't quite ready to talk or open up to anyone but in time we would become friends. I was still struggling with everything and all of my loss. I had no more room in my heart to store anymore pain and my whole life was turned upside down. I wished that I was dead and I felt that the family would be better off without me.

    I remember one Sunday morning before going to church I noticed that my mom was very sad on that morning. I could see the pain in her eyes. On that Sunday morning, my heart was full and I was feeling sad and depressed myself; I felt I was dying inside. On that same Sunday morning, my Uncle Nick stopped by just to see how we were doing; he was one of my dad's brothers. After my uncle left, my mom was very sad, and I guessed she was reminded of my dad because I recall my mom threw a bottle of fingernail polish at me that morning, and told me to get out. My heart was already full when my mom told me to get out of her house that morning. I remember feeling so destroyed, and I didn't want my mom to see me crying. I went to church that morning feeling

Wounds
For Love Comes Tragic and Painful

confused and broken inside. I wasn't sure where I was going to go. I had no money and no job at the time. I knew that this was a very hard time for my mom and my family. I just wanted it all to stop – I wanted all the pain and hurt to stop and go away. Even though I was hurting when my mom told me to get out, I didn't blame her. She had every right to be mad; she was going through a tough time in her life. But so was I, but yet I felt I had hurt her. I held back my tears in church and suppressed all of what I was feeling inside; it felt like the weight of the whole world was on my shoulder. I knew it was time for me to leave my mom's house. I had caused enough problems for her and the family.

I had to find a job, but back then there weren't any jobs in this little small town. It was time for me to take care of myself. After church, I came home and I laid down for a while. I was feeling depressed and I fell asleep. When I woke up, mom and my siblings had left and I was home alone. The family had gone to my Aunt Helen's house. I called my friend from the hospital, Ken, and told him I needed to leave this place and find a place for myself. I had decided to go to Houston, Texas. I needed to get my life back together if that was possible. He bought my bus ticket and gave me money. He hesitated at first because he said he didn't want to get in trouble with my mom. I felt that it was best for me to leave because I'd caused enough problems for my family, so I got on the bus and headed for Houston. I had family in Texas and I was hoping that I could stay with my aunt and uncle while I looked for a job. My mother had called Ken after I left to find out if he knew where I was. Ken told her that he had taken me to the bus station. When I arrived in Houston, I called my Aunt Martha and Uncle Peter, and they picked me up from the bus station. I was told by my aunt that my mom called looking for me. So I called home when I got over to my Aunt Martha's house. My mom wanted to know why I left home without telling anyone. I felt that I was on my own now. I told my mother that it was best that I left, and besides, she had told me to get out of her house. So I did. I also told my mom that it was time for me to leave and get a fresh start. I knew my mom was having a hard time coping with the loss of my dad, and I didn't want to add to it. I felt with me gone, maybe things would be a little easier for her, and maybe she could begin her healing process without me being there. I recall my grandmother begging me to come back home and telling me that I could live with her. I knew my grandmother was on a fixed income and she lived in a housing project for people on fixed incomes. With that, I didn't want to cause anymore problems. I told my grandmother thank you, but I wasn't coming back home; I was going to try to make a fresh start for myself.

WOUNDS
FOR LOVE COMES TRAGIC AND PAINFUL

I was able to get my first job in Houston while staying with my aunt and uncle. They helped me get on my feet. I got a job working with Aunt Martha at a deli in Downtown Houston, serving breakfast and lunch. My aunt taught me how to ride the Metro bus and I learned how to get around. I remember my uncle would drop me and my aunt off to work in the mornings, and we would ride the bus to get home. I liked riding the bus because I got a chance to see different parts of the city. I was learning how to get around the city very fast riding the bus. Growing up, I'd always wanted to travel when I got older. I always wanted to visit all the beautiful cities that I dreamed about my whole life.

Although I was learning new things in the city, I was far from being healed. I was still dealing with many issues in my life. I was having problems sleeping at night, having many nightmares and bad dreams. I wished they would go away. Even though I was living with my aunt and uncle at the time, they had two kids, and I knew it was not easy for them too. I became more and more angry and bitter with myself. I felt I didn't know how to control the things that were going on in my head. Although I had moved away from home, my problems were far from being over. I was still dealing with the shame, guilt, and humiliation that I had caused my family. I was still struggling with a lot of mental issues that I didn't know how to turn off. This was a very dark place for me. I had not talked to anyone, or told anyone my story of what had happened. I just kept everything bottled up inside of me. I felt I had no one I could trust but God, and I felt like God had forgotten about me. I didn't know how to get my joy, peace, self-esteem, and self-respect back. I was always a very high-spirited person, and I would speak my mind. I was an easy-going person, too. But now, I was in a place mentally where I did not know me anymore; nothing felt right about me and what I was going through.

I wasn't dealing with the loss of everything well: my dad, my daughter, my family, my aunt, my virginity, myself. So to take my mind off of things, I learned my way around the city fast, and then I got a second job. I was very thankful for aunt and uncle letting me stay with them until I was able to get back on my feet. Finally, I saved enough money to move out and get my own apartment. I was still having problems sleeping at night with all the bad dreams and flashbacks about what my husband had did to me. Although I knew my problem was far from being over, I was finally able to get my divorce the following year.

WOUNDS
FOR LOVE COMES TRAGIC AND PAINFUL

Now I was waiting for my big day in court for the killing of my dad. I wanted Adam to pay for what he did to me and my family. I wanted to be there so he could see my face when I would testify. I was looking forward to that day. I wanted this to be my last time to ever see him again, once they take him to jail. That would be my revenge; I wanted him to suffer in jail like he had made me suffer as a prisoner in my own skin everyday for the last nine months. I thought finally that little voice inside of my head that had been silent for so long would finally go away so I could have peace.

But that didn't happen. I was so disappointed when I learned that I wasn't going to have my day in court. I was told by my mom that my ex-husband had pleaded guilty to manslaughter. I was outraged about the whole situation. I couldn't believe what my mom was telling me. I had a hard time processing the fact that I wasn't going to get my day in court to speak out about the abuse and the killing. No one spoke out on behalf of my dad. I was very angry; I felt that this wasn't fair. I had blamed myself for my dad's death and I didn't even get to speak out. That made me more bitter toward my ex-husband. He had taken the easy way out. How pathetic! I felt cheated for all the hell he put me though. I was still paying for a lot of the things he did, and it wasn't easy for me to erase the mental and physical abuse. Back then, there weren't a lot of support groups for abuse or battered women like myself.

I had moved to Houston thinking that the pain would go away, but it didn't. I just kept facing one problem after another. I found myself running from my problems. I met a man some years later. His name was Bob. He would talk to me when I was cleaning the tables every morning as he was eating his breakfast. I noticed that Bob seemed to be interested in me at the time. After some months, I would end up marrying Bob and moving to Chicago. On the outside everything seemed normal, but on the inside, I was dying and my heart hadn't been repaired. My mind was still destroying me, and the last thing I needed was another man in my life at the time. I became Bob's wife, but he and I would later end our marriage because I still had a long way to go with my healing and Bob committed adultery repeatedly in our relationship. A few years later, I met another man and after we became friends some months later, we were married. He was a military man and later I found out that he was addicted to drugs and using our marriage as a cover-up for his addiction. So he and I didn't work out either. After that, there were no more husbands, just messed up relationships with men. I also tried committing suicide several times, and even tried getting myself killed on the streets of Chicago. But God wouldn't allow anyone to kill me or me to

Wounds
For Love Comes Tragic and Painful

kill myself. That is when I started visiting the cemetery. I found myself there when I went home to visit my family. They would say things that hurt my feelings and I would take a drive to the cemetery to visit my dad and my daughter. I knew I could always find peace there.

I remember there was one time when I visited my mother's house and I was just tired of holding everything inside. I recalled saying some mean and hurtful things back to my family that day, even using the 'B' word again in front of my mother to my sister. I had promised a long time ago that I would never do that again. Although I wasn't proud of what I did, I just went on and left the house again to go back to Texas without saying anything else to them.

I or my family, to my knowledge, never had any counseling or help to process what we all had been through. As a result of my cutting and bruising myself, that is, my continued blaming myself for my father's death, I became severely depressed, suicidal, and stricken with disease and sickness. I tried to live a normal life, after getting married several times. But none of my relationships worked; I just kept going from place to place trying to get along with me.

In 2008, after several years of experiencing vision and eye disorders, hearing problems, memory loss, and chronic body pains and physical imbalance, I went to see a doctor along with my mother. I was diagnosed with Multiple Sclerosis, a disease of the central nervous system that affects the brain and spinal cord. Since then, my life has not been the same. I had held a wonderful job as a Retail Manager in a large specialty retail chain store for many years, but I lost my job due to the symptoms I was having at work. The disease caused me to have loss of concentration, limb weaknesses, visual disturbances, and muscle spasms, loss of sensation, dizziness, and depression. I didn't know anything about the Americans with Disabilities Act, so I quit my job, feeling overwhelmed being sick, on medication, and under so much pressure all the time. I was still after nearly thirty years later, dealing with the nightmares, grief, and loss.

In the Bible there is a story of a woman caught in adultery. She was guilty of sleeping around with men other than her husband. Some of her accusers brought her to Jesus to see what He would say about her. In those days, the people would kill any whores if they found them in the city. When Jesus saw through their motives, He looked at her accusers and said, *"Let him who is without sin, cast the first stone upon her."* Then all of them one by one quietly turned and

WOUNDS
FOR LOVE COMES TRAGIC AND PAINFUL

walked away. They slipped back into the crowd. When Jesus looked up, none of the accusers had stayed. They were all gone. He looked over at the woman and said, *"Woman, where are your accusers? Has any man accused you?"* To this she said, *"No Lord, not one."* So Jesus said, *"Then neither do I. Go and sin no more."*

In this story there was a guilty woman who deserved to be beaten to death according to law. Yet, none of her accusers could throw out the first stone because they were all guilty themselves. In my story, there were no accusers – not even one man who could say I had slept with him before my marriage to my first husband, yet my husband savagely beat and raped me because he thought I had. I saved myself for the one who I believed to be my true love. Yet, I was beaten, taunted, and finally robbed by the death of my father. In the Scriptures, Jesus saw the condition of the woman, and forgave her. I wondered if I could ever be forgiven and set free too.

Rolling Away the Stone

Why did I need forgiveness? I didn't do anything! He hurt me! This is how I felt. But over the years, I came to see that I was in a downward spiral all started by sin. The sins of my husband had caused me to sin years later, and keep sinning. All of my life had been affected by those terrible memories. I tried drugs; I tried alcohol; I tried killing myself, and I tried sleeping around with men later. Sin had created wounds on the walls of my mind, so much so, that thirty years later, I was still being affected. I had lost five children through miscarriage, three husbands, a career, my health, my virginity, and my livelihood. Now I was sick, depressed, disabled, suicidal, and steadily going down. I just had to get free!

God connected me with a wonderful woman in Louisiana, a woman I call my Godmother, because she has been like a handmaiden leading me to my Lord to open me up to forgiveness, and a new life over the years. She has patiently been there spiritually and physically for me, providing a home and a reason to keep coming back to God for all the questions of my purpose. I know there is a reason God enabled me to live through all the trauma, and I have determined to find out what that purpose is. That is what keeps me going every day.

Wounds
For Love Comes Tragic and Painful

The road has not been easy. But I am on my pathway to recovery. I discovered that I had suppressed so much of my childhood from the traumatic experience. The disease I had attacked my memory. It literally hurt for me to recall things so I just kept them buried down at the cemetery where my dad, little girl, and loved ones were buried. You may notice in this book that I used the words, *"I recall,"* and *"I remember"* a lot. That is because I could not remember for a while all of the things that had happened to me. The nightmares of everything that had happened throughout those traumatic months that followed my wedding night, years later caused me to begin suppressing my memories.

As the stones of grief, loss, sickness, condemnation, disease, and failure, started being rolled away, I believe it was nothing but the personal healing loving hand of Jesus Christ that touched my life and made me able to share this story. It is His care, His touch, His love that healed me. There is so much more that happened to me after those incidents that I did not write in this book; it just would have been too overwhelming. I hope that by reading this book other young women and older ones too will not suffer the same situation. I should have never stayed in that abusive situation; it was doomed from the start. But because of my lack of understanding of who I was, whose I was, and what I deserved, I was willing to give an abusive situation a chance at ruining my life, and terrorizing my family. I cannot stress the words, *"Get out!"* enough. All people, not just young women, but young men and older ones too need to learn how to conquer their issues before marriage. You do not know who you are, until you can learn to love yourself without hating or harming someone else! That goes for everyone – all of us!

Soul wounds are real, and they exist in all of us. Most people will never admit that they have them. We get soul wounds from sin. The sins of others and the sins we inflict upon ourselves, both create soul wounds. I learned that it doesn't matter where the sin comes from, or who is to blame, sin will still destroy no matter what – because that is what sin does. Sin is no respecter of persons; it takes out good persons as well as bad persons. It takes the Light of Jesus Christ to deal with sin and heal the soul wounds (Souza, 2010). Additionally, it takes forgiveness and repentance to be healed of the soul wounds. It didn't matter that I did not kill my dad; the sin of my dad being killed caused me to sin years and years after his death. People are getting hurt and killed all because they have been wounded in their souls. There are even people singing, preaching, sitting on the pews, and working in the church every Sunday with huge wounds. I know because I have lived with them and have been one of those people myself. Before they

Wounds
For Love Comes Tragic and Painful

deal with their issues, they secretly struggle. I had to learn how to forgive the man that hurt me, killed my dad, and ruined me and my family's life for those thirty years. He never asked me or my family for forgiveness; in fact, I saw him in church years later and he acted like nothing ever happened. But I was able to forgive him within myself.

    The wounds on my soul were created by sin (Souza, 2010) and they almost took out my entire life. I am so glad that there is a God who knows me and understands my pain, and He forever lives to see that I am accepted by Him. I didn't choose Him, He chose me! That's why Jesus Christ is my hero; He healed my broken heart! He is the One who came after my father was gone. He is the One who rolled away my stone.

REFERENCES

Souza, Katie., *The Glory Light of Jesus Heals Your Soul*, Expected End Ministries, 2010. Teaching Series at www.ExpectedEndMinistries.com

WOUNDED FOR ME

ABOUT THE AUTHOR

Author Laura Doucet's personal testimony is that her biological father was stabbed and fatally wounded while saving her life. This is the same way she views her Lord and Savior, Jesus Christ.

An experienced Retail Branch Manager of a Specialty Store for over 20 years, Laura was born in Lafayette, Louisiana and grew up in the small town of Ville Platte with her five sisters and one brother. At the age of 17, while still a virgin bride on her honeymoon night, Laura was savagely raped at knifepoint and brutally beaten by her groom, a young man she had dated without having sex or any signs of complications in their relationship for three years prior to their marriage. In the nine months that followed their wedding night, Laura's nightmare escalated to the worst of tragedies. As a result, her

WOUNDS
FOR LOVE COMES TRAGIC AND PAINFUL

entire life was marked by the events that followed their wedding. Laura suffered a nervous breakdown and lived in torment, guilt, shame, and grief for over thirty years. While she struggled to make sense out of her life and the grief suffered by her and her family, Laura suppressed her memories and emotions from that traumatic experience. ***Wounds: For Love Comes Tragic and Painful*** is her story of rising from the ashes of grief, bitterness, unforgiveness, and living amongst the tombs to find the love, peace, and resurrection power of Jesus Christ.

Laura shares her lessons learned and the love of Christ at conferences, meetings, business functions, community events and wherever relationship addiction, domestic violence, unhealthy marriages, and abuse are prevalent.

For bookings, contact:
Laura Doucet at www.LauraBook.com
Phone (281) 731-1093
E-mail: LauraBook@Live.com

Contributing Writer & Consultant
Merle Ray
Phone (281) 827-4396
E-mail: mhray@noblegroups.com
Websites: www.WordToWin.com
            www.NobleGroups.com
            www.MyBestSeller.org

CPSIA information can be obtained at www.ICGtesting.com
Printed in the USA
LVOW090331070612

285041LV00002B/52/P